Creative Layout
Perspective for Artists

Featuring the art and techniques of Joko Budiono, Thomas Denmark, and Leandro Ng

Wei-chiun Chiang

Pearson Custom Publishing

Cover design by Joko Budiono, Thomas Denmark, and Leandro Ng.

All art contained in this book created by Joko Budiono, Thomas Denmark, and Leandro Ng.

Printed in the United States of America

10 9 8 7 6 5 4 3 2 1

Please visit our web site at www.pearsoncustom.com

ISBN 0–536–70526–7

BA 996026

PEARSON CUSTOM PUBLISHING
75 Arlington Street, Suite 300, Boston, MA 02116
A Pearson Education Company

Introduction

It is often mentioned in art instruction books that the authors, who are usually teachers, learned more from the students by being teachers. It seems cliche' to say that Tom, Leandro and I learned more about perspective drawing by teaching it to our wonderful students. Every author of an art book mentions this, so it seems "dated" or old fashioned to say it.

Now hold that thought.

We were trying to make a different kind of perspective book. A book both friendly yet complex at the same time. A book that covers large ranges of perspective, layout and most of all useful for creating representational art work. Useful was the key word that we tried to follow. I lost count of how many hours and drawings we did to cover everything we could think of to make this book "useful"; from the variation of subject matter, to the variation of perspective and layout. In the book we even included Isometric drawing in depth, when Isometric was not part of linear perspective. But "useful " was the key word, and isometric drawing was very useful.

As we went along creating this book and teaching at the same time, we began to select and discard a lot of material. Every time the students struggled on a particular area, we looked in to it with a magnifying glass. We asked ourselves: were they struggling because of how complex the problem was? Or were they struggling because in the back of their mind there was a question: "Am I going to use this in the future?" If the second question was the one that the students wondered, then we, as teachers, had to ask the same question. "Are they going to use this in the future?" If the answer was no, then that part would end up in the editing room floor. Moreover if the students told us that they wanted to draw like "that", and pointed to an actual landscape, cityscape or other 3-dimensional thing for that matter, we as teachers had to provide every step to build their drawings to what ever they pointed at. Because it was "useful" for them.

So more than we want to admit, We actually learned more from our students just by teaching them. We were learning to be better teachers, and in this case better authors. We were learning that we were "dated" just like those other writers before us, and proud of it. Without our students, we could not have made this book. So thank you all.

Joko "The Dude" Budiono
April 17, 2002
San Francisco Ca

Dedicated to our students
-for asking such good questions, and turning in such inspiring work.

Special thanks to:

-Paul Nowicky: for the ideas, input and critiques all those years.
-Jim Freed and Tim Evatt: for the good intentions.
-John Poon: for the support and understanding of how busy we could be.
-Molly Mendoza: for putting up with our mess.
-Farida my mom and Soebekty my Dad (Joko's): for ... you know why. I hope I did good Dad.
-Kimmo Ng and Siu Ling Chang Ng (Leandro's): for raising the big guy.
-Avon and Darlene Young (Tom's): for raising a kid not like the others.
-Ellen Supple: for the business connection.
-Our Publisher: Thomas Biondi: for believing in us.
-Anh Lai: For making Leandro do his work.
-Molly Nardone: for not letting Joko quit this project.
-Insio Che and Karen Tsui: for their kindness.
-Walden Wong: for the friendship.
-Barbara Bradley: for shaping our ability.
-Gordon Silveria: for the educational support.
-Melissa Marshal: for the support of us as teachers.
-The best art instructors in the world: Craig Nelson, Zhao Ming Wu, Kazuhiko Sano,
 Bill Maughan, Bill Sanches, Thomas Marsh and all the wonderful instructors we
 came across during all these years.
-Elisa Stephens: for a school with such wonderful students.

To view more of the authors' work online:
www.workshopcrew.com
www.denmarkstudio.com

Creative Layout
Perspective for Artists

Table of Contents

Equipment and techniques used in this book

30°/60°/90° triangle with beveled inking edge.
18" metal ruler
11" x 14" tracing paper
11" x 14" marker paper
11" x 14" smooth bristol paper
8B pencil
Carbon pencil
Black colored pencil

Black soft pastel
Gray Markers, values 10% to Black
Fine black ball point pen
Fine and thick tipped black markers
Kneaded eraser
Electric eraser
Adobe Photoshop
6" x 9" Wacom tablet
Adobe Illustrator

Dry Mediums

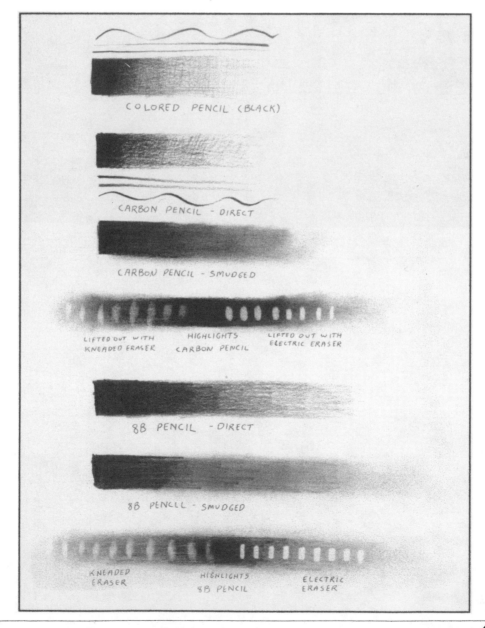

Equipment and techniques used in this book

Markers

BLACK   50%   10%

MARKER - WET INTO WET
   CREATES SOFTER BLENDS

MARKER - GIVEN TIME TO DRY
CREATES CRISPER EDGES

APPLIED SLOWLY - BLEEDS

APPLIED QUICKLY - CRISP

FADED OUT WITH A COLORLESS BLENDER

COMBINE A FINE INK PEN WITH MARKER
TO CREATE INTERESTING TEXTURE AND DETAILS

Pen and Ink Mediums

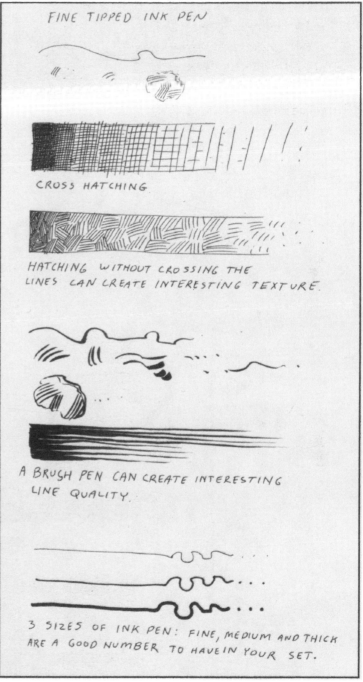

FINE TIPPED INK PEN

CROSS HATCHING

HATCHING WITHOUT CROSSING THE
LINES CAN CREATE INTERESTING TEXTURE.

A BRUSH PEN CAN CREATE INTERESTING
LINE QUALITY.

3 SIZES OF INK PEN: FINE, MEDIUM AND THICK
ARE A GOOD NUMBER TO HAVE IN YOUR SET.

Chapter 1: Isometric

The world in parallel dimensions...

Isometric drawing is used in product design, engineering, concept artwork and often in popular video games where a top down view that does not "distort" is needed.

If you look out your window you will notice that things in the distance appear much smaller than they really are. This may seem like an obvious point, but before the Renaissance, artists did not utilize this principle in their drawings, and would often draw figures in the distance the same size, or larger than figures in the foreground. This created the illusion that distant figures were giants. This happened particularly in the case of royalty, who of course could not possibly be drawn smaller than a commoner!

In an isometric drawing we ignore this basic fact, called diminution, and draw things as if they remain the same size no matter how far they are from your eye.

This quality, that measurements remain the same, is what makes Isometric perspective such a powerful tool for design. Engineers, 3d Modellers, mold makers and many others all rely on Isometric drawings for precision in their craft.

Isometric drawing represents three-dimensions on a two-dimensional surface (your drawing). These dimensions are X: Height, Y: Width, and Z: Depth.

In order to master Isometric drawing, you will need to remember these three fundamental principles:

1. All parallel lines remain parallel

2. All lines are based on a 120° grid.

3. There is no diminution (things do not get smaller in the distance)

A 30°/60°/90° triangle is the ideal tool to aid you in drawing in an Isometric view. Also Isometric grids are provided at the end of this chapter that you can use to assist in drawing in this view.

Isometric Theory

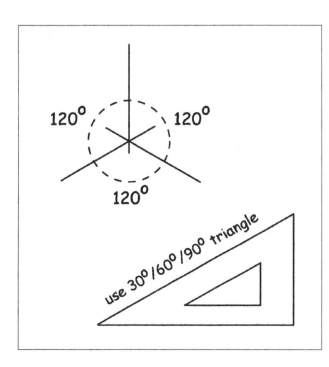

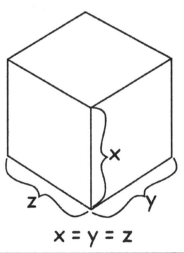

proportions remain of equal measure, objects do not become smaller in the distance

x = y = z

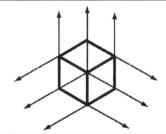

lines on the same axis remain parallel

Chapter 1

Any circle viewed at an angle appears as an ellipse.

Drawing ellipses in isometric view will introduce you to the fundamental principles of drawing ellipses in any perspective.

First we take a perfect square and subdivide the square. To subdivide draw a line across the square from one corner to the opposite corner. Then do the same from the other corners. The point where the lines meet is the center of the box. You can now use this center point as a reference to draw lines across the center of the box. These become guidelines to aid in drawing your ellipse.

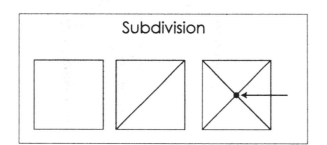

Subdivision

Isometric Ellipses

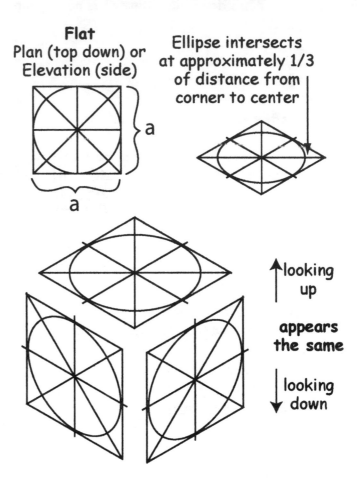

Flat
Plan (top down) or Elevation (side)

a

a

Ellipse intersects at approximately 1/3 of distance from corner to center

↑ looking up

appears the same

↓ looking down

The center of a box is a useful reference point that you will use in a variety of methods discussed later in this book. As an example, in the illustration below it is used to align an ellipse that is set within and back from the larger ellipse to create a hubcap for a car wheel.

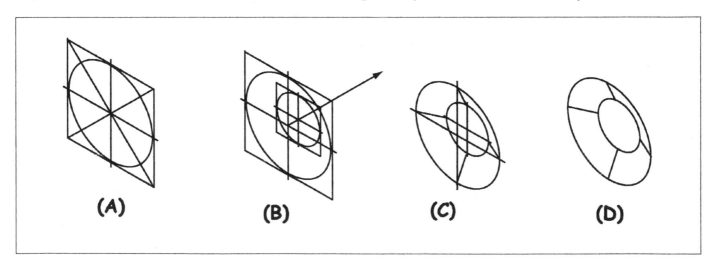

(A)   (B)   (C)   (D)

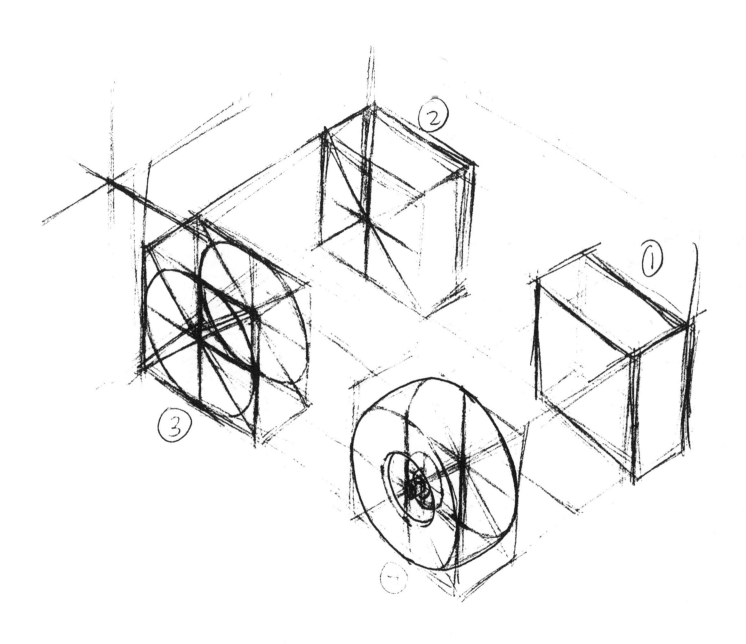

These are simple geometric shapes that could be used as a foundation to build more complex objects or structures.

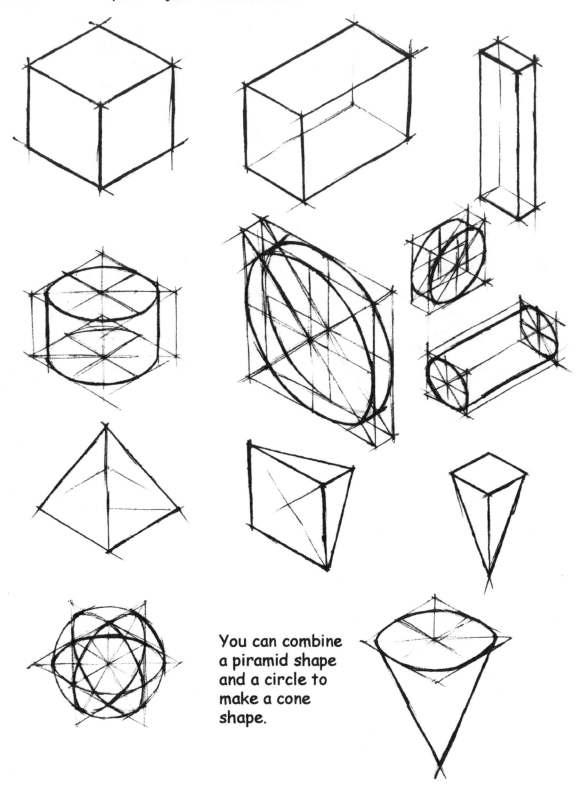

You can combine a piramid shape and a circle to make a cone shape.

STILL LIFE WITH PARALLEL LINES

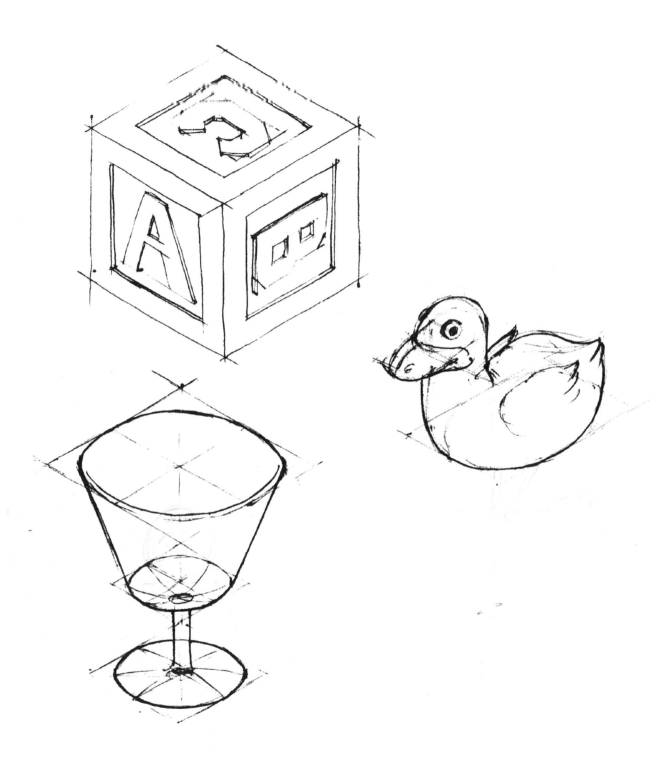

Chapter 1

BUILDING THINGS

STEP 1 :

A CAR BASICALY IS
2 BOXES ONE
ON TOP OF
ANOTHER

STEP 2 :

INDICATE WHERE
ARE THE TIRES
WOULD BE

STEP 3 :

CARVE THE ACTUAL
SHAPE FROM THE
MAJOR BOXES

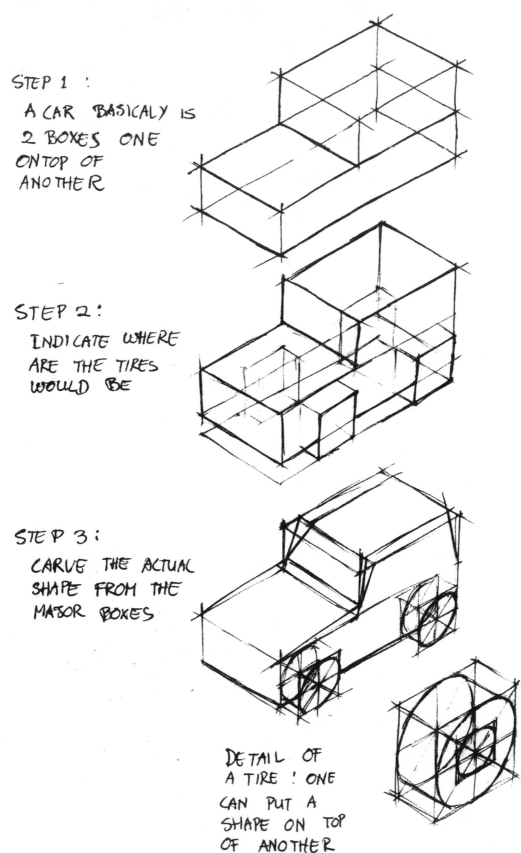

DETAIL OF
A TIRE ! ONE
CAN PUT A
SHAPE ON TOP
OF ANOTHER

STEP 4:

PUTTING DETAIL
WHICH CAN BE:

a) SMALLER SHAPES
AND FORMS

OR

b) TEXTURE:
IN THIS CASE
THE NUMBER
1 ON THE SIDE
OF THE CAR

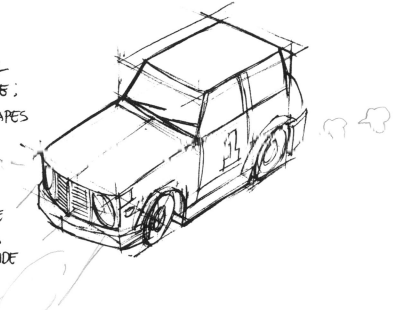

NOW WE WILL DO THE SAME THING: BUILDING A CAR WITH
THE ENVIRONMENT BY USING PARALLEL LINES

Chapter 1

Step by step Isometris drawing

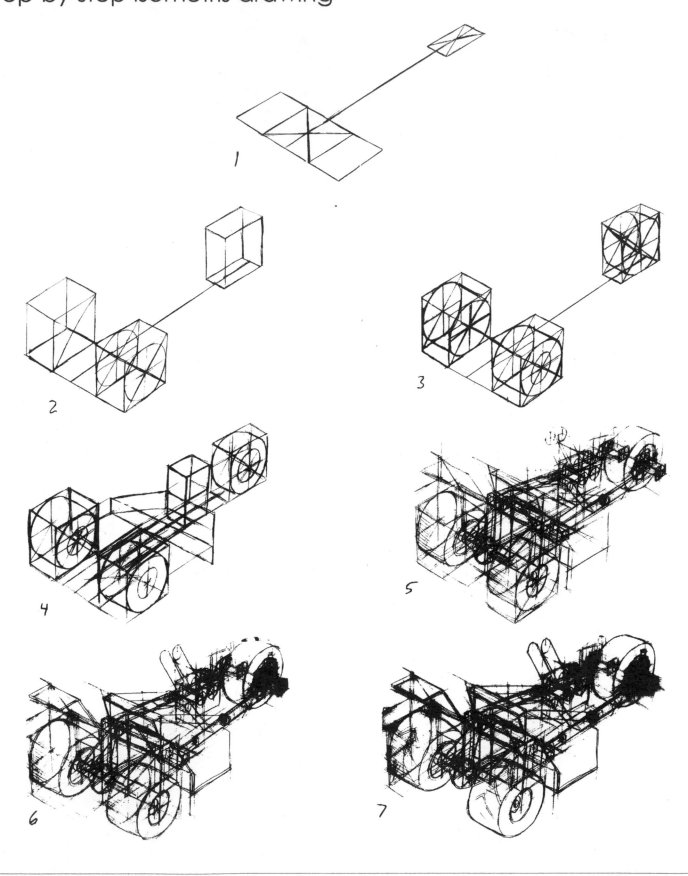

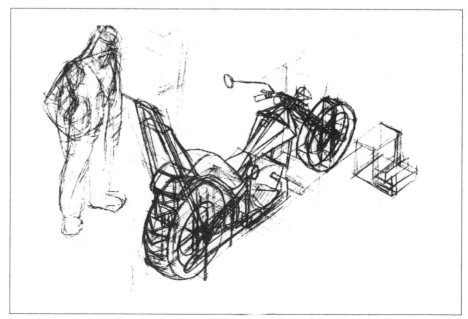

Orthographic
Figures

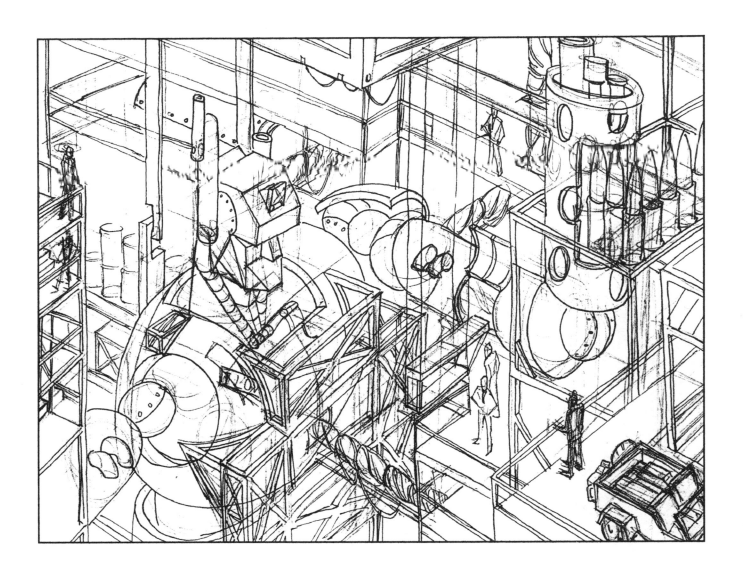

Organic and Mechanic;
Characters using Isometric

Chapter 1

Isometric Looking Up

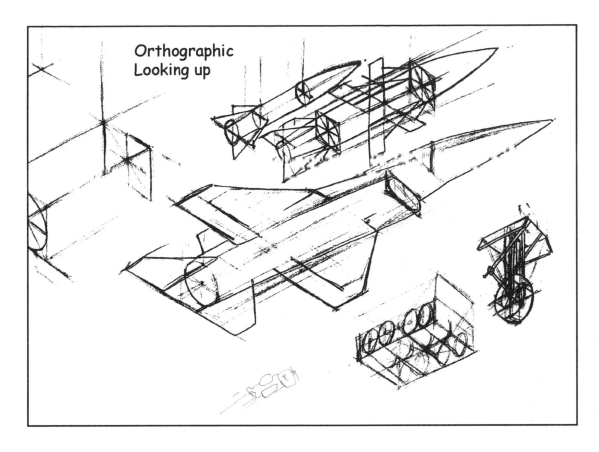

Orthographic
Looking up

This side up

This side up

The world in parallel dimensions, illuminated...

Calculating cast shadows in perspective is one of the most rewarding drawing skills you can have. At first glance the theory may seem complicated, but it is in fact quite simple. This chapter covers the two basic types of light sources, local light (like a lamp on a desk, or street light) and sunlight. There are only two principles you will need to understand in order to calculate cast shadows like a pro.

1. Angle of light from the light source to the top of the object casting the shadow

2. Direction of light from the plan of the light to the base of the object casting the shadow.

The plan of the light is the spot on the ground that the light source is over. "Ground" is whatever plane the cast shadow is falling on.

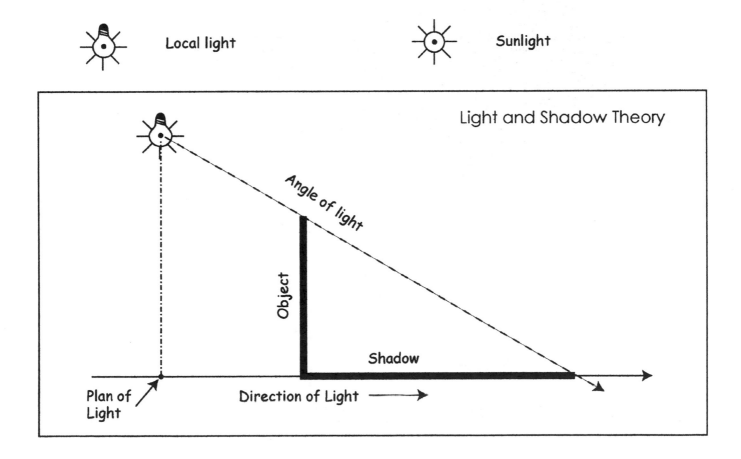

Local light

Sunlight

Light and Shadow Theory

Angle of light

Object

Shadow

Plan of Light

Direction of Light ⟶

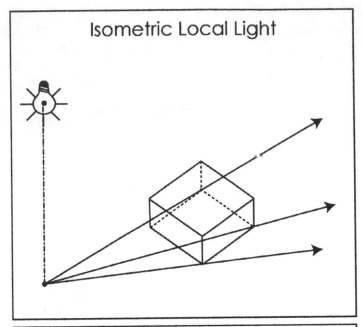

Isometric Local Light

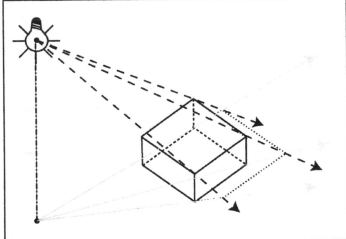

Local Light

(1) Prepare a finished Isometric line drawing.

(2) Determine the Plan of the light, and the location of the light source.

(3) Apply the Direction of light from the Plan of the light, and Angle of light from the light source on every vertical line. Simplify complex shapes to a stick, plane, box, cylinder, pyramid or cone.

(5) Apply the Direction of light on all vertical planes, and the Angle of light on every line that is perpendicular to the side plane.

(6) Block both form and cast shadow with the same value. Form shadow starts where the light turns to shadow on the object itself, and finishes where it turns or faces back to the light again.

(7) Apply Atmospheric perspective (darker *shadows* closer to the viewer, lighter/less contrast farther away).

Isometric Sun Light

Angle and direction of Light are Constant

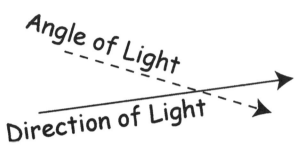

Angle of Light

Direction of Light

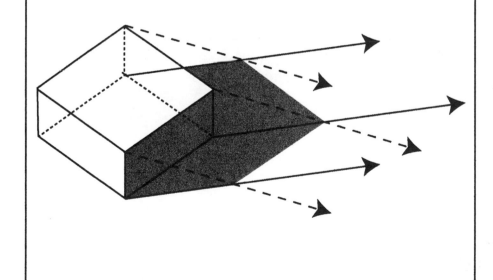

Sunlight
(1) Prepare a finished Isometric line drawing.
(2) Determine the Direction of the Sunlight and the Angle of Sunlight, this is up to you, but once you establish it, the angle and direction must remain constant.
(3) You may need to figure out the Direction of Sunlight on the vertical plane using an Isometric box.
(4) Apply the Direction of Sunlight and Angle of Sunlight on every vertical line. Simplify complex shapes to a stick, plane, box, cylinder, pyramid or cone.
(5) Apply the Direction of Sunlight on all vertical planes, and the Angle of Sunlight on every line that is perpendicular to the side plane.
(6) Block both form and cast shadow with the same value. Form shadow starts where the light turns to shadow on the object itself, and finishes where it turns or faces back to the light again.
(7) Apply Atmospheric perspective (darker *shadows* closer to the viewer, lighter/less contrast farther away).

Isometric Light and Shadow
Objects not touching ground plane

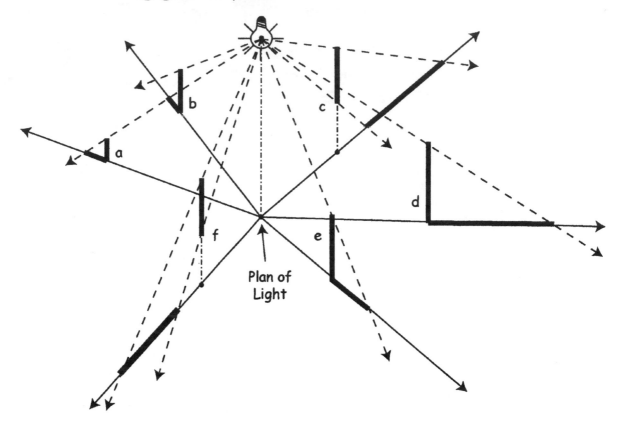

Plan of
Light

Objects (c) and (f) are not touching the ground plane.

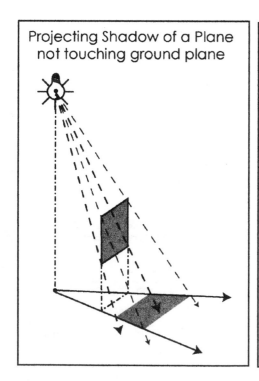

Projecting Shadow of a Plane
not touching ground plane

Projecting Shadow of a Box
not touching ground plane

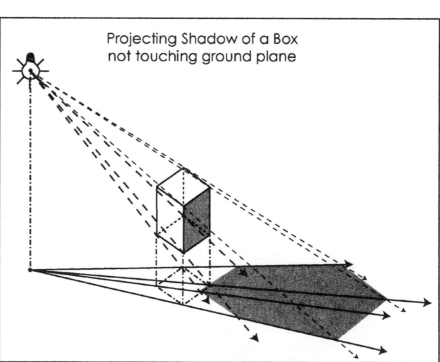

Cast Shadow on Different Planes

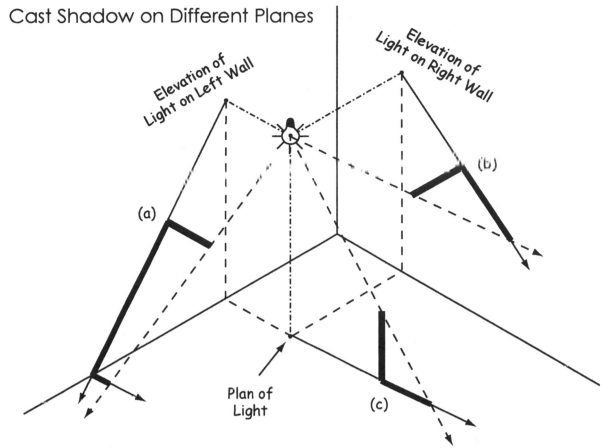

Object (a) is Perpendicular to the Left Wall. Object (b) is Perpendicular to the Right Wall
Object (c) is Perpendicular to the Ground Plane

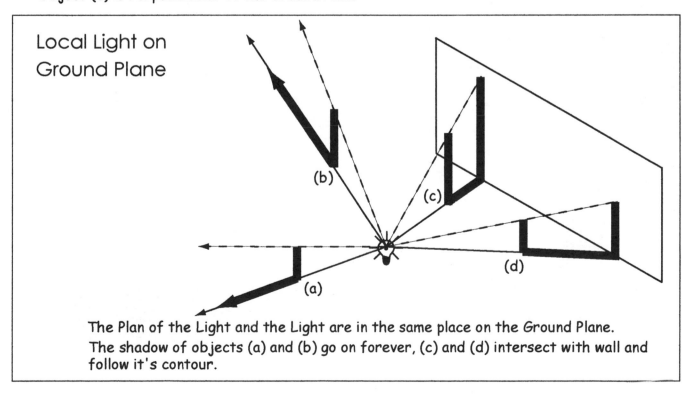

Local Light on Ground Plane

The Plan of the Light and the Light are in the same place on the Ground Plane.
The shadow of objects (a) and (b) go on forever, (c) and (d) intersect with wall and
follow it's contour.

Chapter 2

Cast Shadow on Different Planes Which are Parallel to Ground Plane

Sunlight

Local Light

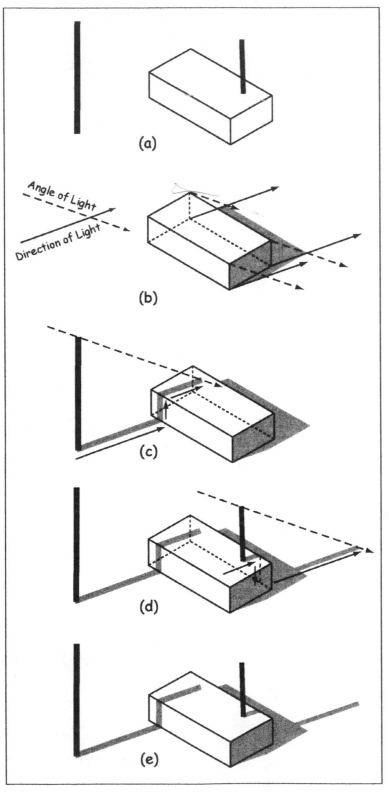

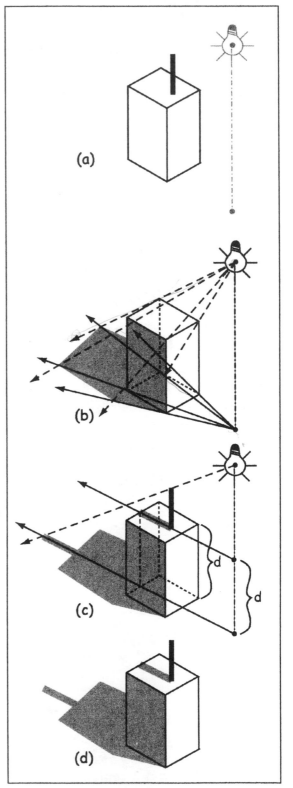

Sunlight Cast Shadows on Different Planes
(other than planes that are parallel with Ground Plane)

1)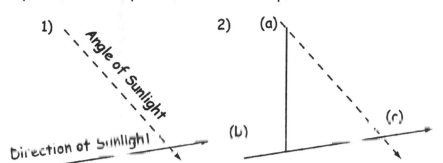

Angle of Sunlight

Direction of Sunlight

2) (a) (b) (c)

3) (a) (b) (c)

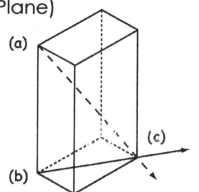

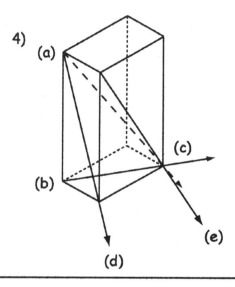

1) Determine the Direction and Angle of Sunlight.

2) Connect a vertical line anywhere between the Direction and Angle before the two meet.

3) Make an Isometric box connecting (a), (b) and (c). The line connecting (b) and (c) is a diagonal line on the Ground Plane.

4) Transfer the Angle of Sunlight to all the Isometric box Elevation planes. Now you have the new direction of Sunlight on the other two vertical planes (d) and (e).

4) (a) (b) (c) (d) (e)

The Angle of Sunlight remains the same for (A), (B) and (C).

The Direction of Sunlight for (B) and (C) uses diagonal line from (a) to (d) above.

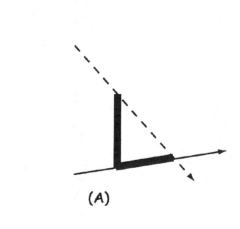

(A)

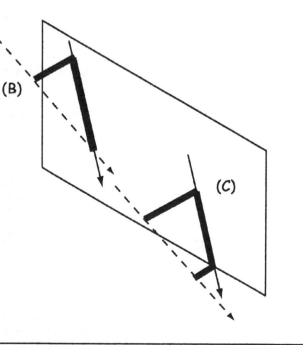

(B)

(C)

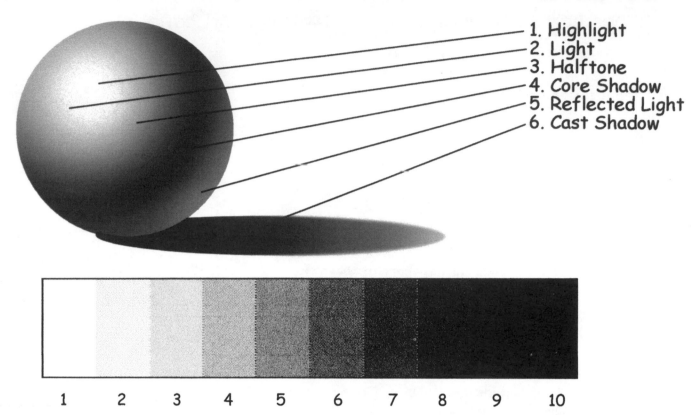

1. Highlight
2. Light
3. Halftone
4. Core Shadow
5. Reflected Light
6. Cast Shadow

1	2	3	4	5	6	7	8	9	10

Six Basic Values

Imagine that all values are simplified onto a scale from 1 to 10. 1 being pure white, 5 being middle gray and 10 being pure black. This is only a hypothetical framework to assist you in better rendering the light and shadow in your drawing. Every lighting situation is different, but in general the six basic values fall on this scale as follows:

1. Highlight= 1
2. Light= 2-3
3. Halftone= 4-6
4. Core shadow= 9-10
5. Reflected light=6-8
6. Cast shadow= 9-10 nearest the object, fading to 7-8 or lighter.

Furthermore the values have an edge quality, which is a relationship of soft (blurry) to sharp (crisp). In general the 6 basic values have these edge qualities:

Highlight is generally sharp, and usually has a tail or an edge that is softer.

Light, halftone, core shadow and reflected light usually have a soft, seamless gradation from light to dark.

Cast shadow is sharp, particularly near the object casting the shadow and tends to get softer and lighter as it moves away from the object. It is this contrast of soft core shadow (often referred to as form shadow, because it creates the illusion of form) and hard cast shadow that most gives a drawing three-dimensional solidity.

Local Tone

The local tone of an object is its actual value, for example a white sheet of paper has a local tone of value 1 or 2, while a black cloth might have a local tone of value 9 or 10. The local tone can have an effect on all of the Six Basic Values described above, making them overall darker or lighter.

Prepare a finished Isometric drawing.

Determine the plan of the light and the location of the light source.

See "cast shadow on different planes" and determine the elevation of light on the right wall, and the elevation of light on the left wall.

See "cast shadow on different planes" to calculate the form and cast shadows.

Chapter 2

Block the cast shadows and the form shadows with one value. The point here is too simplify. Use a dark value (7 or darker on the value scale).

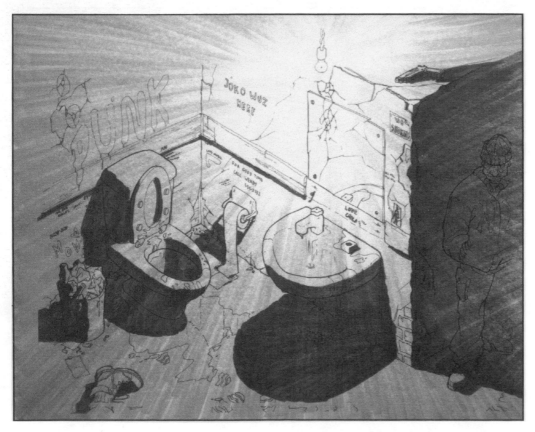

Apply value changes (gradation) from the light source out. Don't lose your separation of dark and light. The values in the light range from 1 to 5, while those in the shadow range from 6 to 10.

Apply soft edges, core shadows, darker cast shadows, local tones and high lights to the work.

See if you can find the shadow that the artist missed.

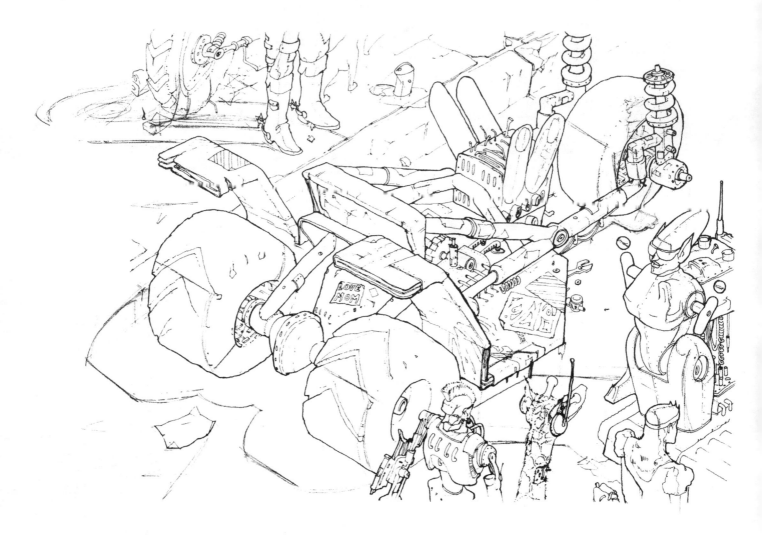

Prepare the finished Isometric drawing.

Determine the direction of the sunlight and the angle of the sunlight. In this case the direction comes from the right side of the picture (straight from the right), and the angle is 45 degrees from the top.

Apply the Direction of the sunlight to the bottom of the objects that touch the ground and the Angle of the sunlight to the top of the objects, and mark the intersections.

Block the form shadows (the shadows on the object itself), and the cast shadows (the shadows that cast to other objects).

Block the form and the cast shadows with the same value.

Chapter 2

Apply soft eges, core shadows and darker cast shadows

Creative Layout

Apply local tone on the major areas.

Finish: Apply local tones on small areas and high lights (details).

For the drawing below, the Direction of the sun comes from straight from the left, and the angle of the sun comes from about 45 degrees from the top.

Prepare the finished Isometric line drawing.

Creative Layout

Determine the Direction of the sunlight and the angle of the sunlight

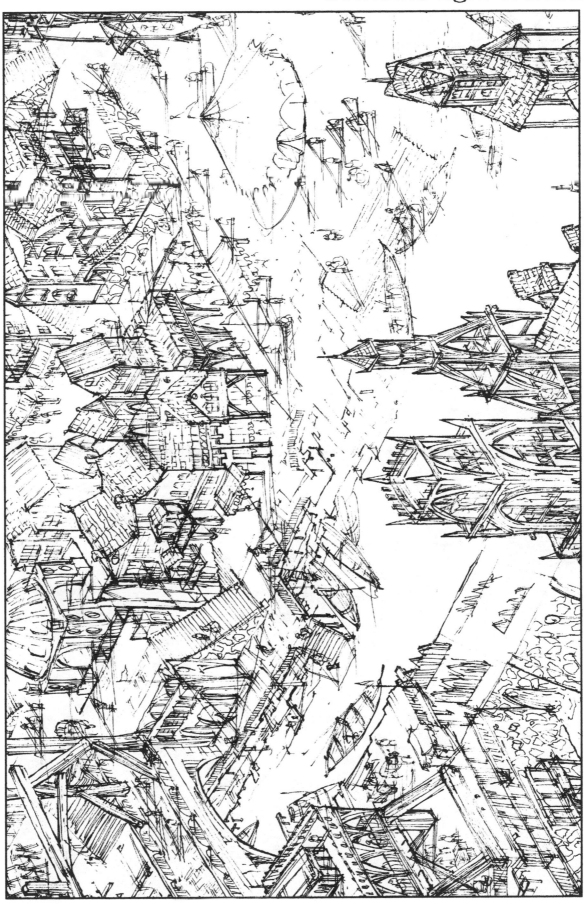

Block the form and the cast shadow with the same value.

Apply atmospheric perspective and details.

Isometric drawing with one local light source (see "local light on ground plane").

Isometric drawing with multiple local light sources.

Chapter 3: Atmospheric Perspective

The world in shades of gray...

Creative Layout

Atmospheric perspective is the principle that objects farther away appear to be diffused by the atmosphere, compared to objects that are closer and appear sharper because there is less diffusion from the atmosphere.

In atmospheric perspective the solutions are not always as precise as they are in linear perspective, but there are good guidelines to help you achieve depth in your drawing through the use of value, edges and line. This theory of atmospheric perspective relies on relationships compared to one another create the illusion of depth.

Relationships can seem more subjective when analyzed and can change depending on the context of the drawing. For example a sharper edge in relation to a softer edge will appear to be closer. Although you can choose to blur things in the foreground and sharpen details in the middleground to create a focal point.

Atmospheric Theory - Relationships

Closer	Farther
Sharper Edges	Softer Edges
Darker Shadows	Lighter Shadows
More Contrast	Less Contrast
More Detail	Less Detail
Larger Shapes	Smaller Shapes
More Value Variation	Less Value Variation
More Form	Less Form
Thicker Line	Thinner Line
More Line Variation	Less Line Variation
More Line Detail	Less Line Detail

Line Quality diagram

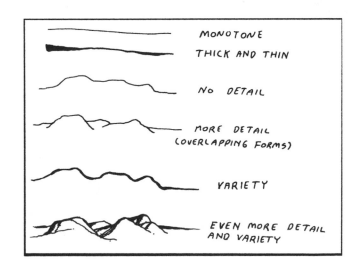

MONOTONE

THICK AND THIN

NO DETAIL

MORE DETAIL
(OVERLAPPING FORMS)

VARIETY

EVEN MORE DETAIL AND VARIETY

Examples of Value and Form

Objects in the foreground
appear to have sharper edges,
while elements in the distance
have softer edges. Shadows
are darker in the foreground
and lighter the further away
from the viewer.

The foreground has more detail,
and shapes tend to be larger
(like the cracks in the mud on
the illustration to the left).

Foreground elements have more
value variation: light, middle
value and dark, and have more
form. While objects in the
distance tend to be more
monotone, and have less form,
appearing more as simple
shapes.

A SINGLE FOCAL POINT WILL ALWAYS MAKE YOUR DRAWING STRONGER. SELECTIVE DETAIL THAT IS SUBORDINATE TO THE FOCAL POINT WORKS BETTER.

WHEN EVERYTHING IS EQUALLY RENDERED THE EYE HAS NO PLACE TO SETTLE. EVERYTHING COMPETES. YET THIS IS THE MOST COMMON MISTAKE. WE OFTEN THINK ADDING MORE DETAIL, OR RENDERING MORE WILL MAKE IT BETTER, BUT IT ACTUALLY RUINS THE COMPOSITION.

MECHANICAL V. ORGANIC

ROUND V. SQUARE

IF YOU KEEP YOUR DRAWING TO 4 OR LESS VALUES IT WILL BE STRONGER.

Chapter 3

SAME SPACING = BORING

UNEQUAL SPACING = MORE INTERESTING

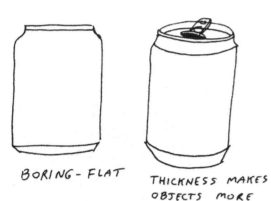

FLAT, NO OVERLAPPING, SAME SPACING MAKES THIS BORING.

BORING - FLAT

THICKNESS MAKES OBJECTS MORE INTERESTING

OVERLAPPING ELEMENTS, THICKNESS AND VARIETY OF SHAPES MAKES THIS MORE INTERESTING.

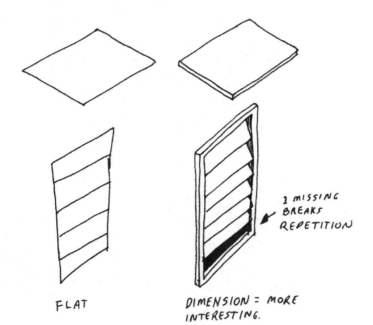

1 MISSING BREAKS REPETITION

FLAT

DIMENSION = MORE INTERESTING.

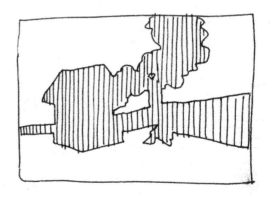

THINK OF COMPOSITION IN TERMS OF NEGATIVE SHAPE. IF IT HAS A VARIETY OF SHAPES: SMALL, MEDIUM AND LARGE IT WILL BE MORE INTERESTING

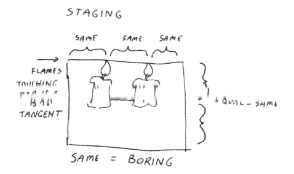

STAGING

SAME   SAME   SAME

FLAMES TOUCHING — BAD TANGENT

EQUAL — SAME

SAME = BORING

LITTLE MORE INTERESTING BUT IMAGE IS STILL BORING.

DIVIDE SPACE INTO LARGE SHAPES AND SMALLER SHAPE

Using line to create atmospheric depth.

Thicker lines give an element in your drawing the appearance of being closer to the viewer's eye. As things go farther back in space you can use thinner and thinner lines to give the illusion that they are farther away. This generally applies to the outline of the object. Thin lines within an object can create the sense of more detail and it will appear closer. The simpler and less defined elements are, the farther away the object will appear.

Line variation, (usually referred to as line quality) is a variety of thick and thin lines. Line quality usually makes an object closer and more visually stimulating. The more monotone or simple the line variation in an object is, the farther away it will appear.

More line detail, which is form overlapping form, particularly on the edges creates the appearance of an object, which is closer or more in focus. The less detail you have in your line, or the less overlapping forms the farther away an object will appear.

The illustration below gives the illusion of a figure in the foreground that is much close with the use of line and atmospheric perspective. There is no linear perspective to create the illusion of depth.

The figure has strong contrast of lights and darks, variety of line (thick and thin), form overlapping form, and more detail compared to the elements in the background.

Chapter 3

The more thumbnail sketches you do before you start your finished drawing, the better your composition will be. When you do a page of thumbnails, rarely is the first one the best one. Yet if you didn't do any thumbnails the first one would be your drawing! It may seem tedious at first, but you'll find once you start sketching out little thumbnails, using simple values and shapes it becomes very addictive. When drawing thumbnails keep these guidelines in mind:

1. Simple values: light, middle value and dark.
2. Simple shapes: small, medium and large.
3. Sameness is boring: create contrast and variety of shapes: ie. round vs. square, or repeating triangles of various sizes and angles.

Chapter 3

Atmosheric perspective - step by step example.

1. Block in the large shapes, working from light values in the distance to darker values in the foreground. At this stage create a simple division of foreground and background.

2. Add more contrast, sharpening edges in the foreground, leaving elements in the background more diffused and less detailed. Further separate the elements in your composition into foreground, middleground and background in order to create as much depth as possible, but be careful not to break up the shapes too much and ending up with a "spotty" composition.

3. Finish your composition with details. Enjoy drawing the details without losing the overall impact of your drawing. It's very easy to get lost in the small stuff, but if you maintain the integrity of your shapes, your composition will be stronger and read better.

Creative Layout

When you do thumbnails, try to vary your light sources and the position of focal points. Be creative!!!!!

Diminuting World...

One Point Perspective Theory

Plan: The floor plan of the object/room (top down view).

Elevation: The wall of the object/room (side view).

Height (h): The distance your eye is from the ground.

Station point (sp): Representation of where your are standing, and the direction you are looking in relation to the object/room.

Picture Plane (pp): an imaginary giant paper/canvas/glass where you will project your object/room to. This can also be considered the surface of your paper you are drawing on.

Ground Line (gl): The line on the ground where you put your picture plane.

Vanishing point (vp): the dot where everything that is parallel to your view goes.

Horizon Line (hl): Eye level (el).

Cone of Vision: a 60∞ angle range that objects still appear normal within your drawing, outside the Cone of Vision objects in your drawing appear distorted.

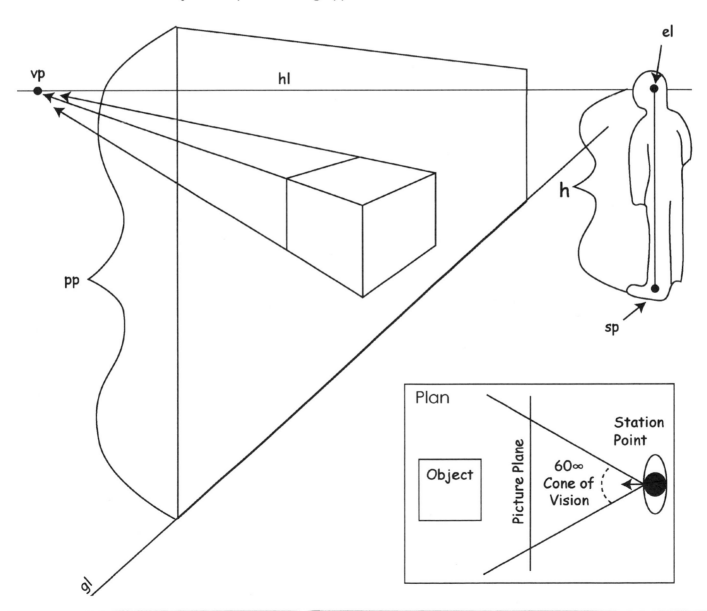

Chapter 4

One Point Perspective Theory
Direct Drawing Step by Step

a) Decide Point-of-View
Choose a view of the object (environment), looking at one side of the object, or parallel to one side of the object. Any other view is not one-point perspective.

In the plan view below there are only 6 views from "a" that are one-point perspective: parallel or perpendicular to the objects. choose one of these views. The other 2 would be looking straight up (called the zenith) or straight down (called the nadir).

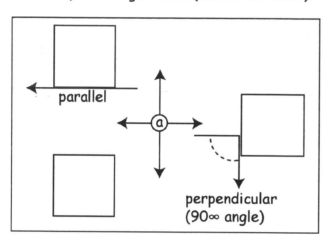

b) Place Vanishing Point:
The picture plane (pp) represents your drawing surface (paper). Place a dot on your paper, anywhere but on the edge or directly in the center (for better composition). This is your one vanishing point.

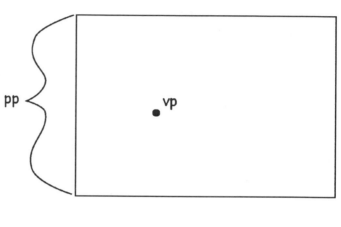

c) Horizon Line:
If you are not looking directly up or down, the vanishing point (vp) is on your horizon line (hl), draw a horizon line.

c) Vanishing Lines:
Draw vanishing lines radiating straight out from vanishing point (vp) to use as guides for your one-point perspective drawing.

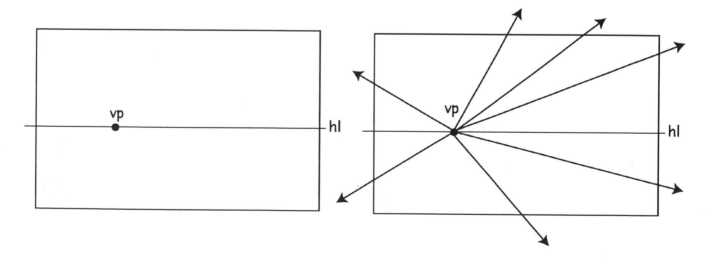

e) Sketch Shapes:
Draw shapes that would be repeated to the vanishing point (vp). Close the shape by repeating it.

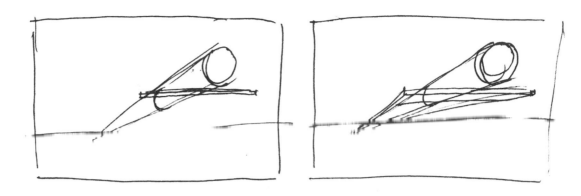

f) Repeat Shapes:
Repeat the shapes until you have the object you want to draw blocked in.

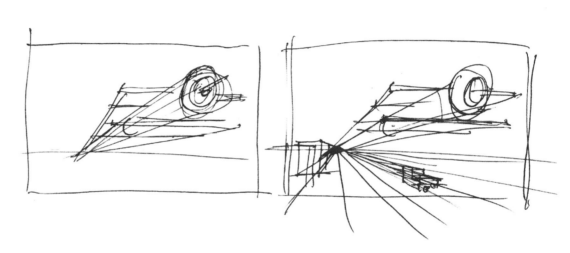

g) Finish:
Finish the drawing by adding smaller shapes and texture.

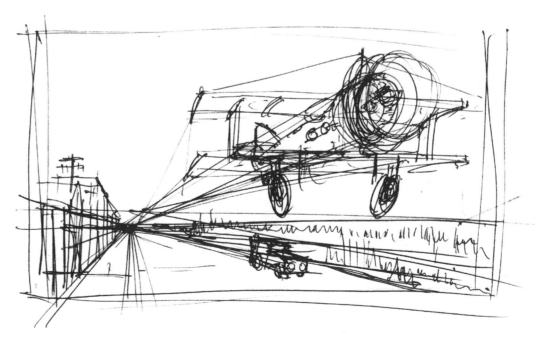

Chapter 4

Equal Shapes and Division

a) Find the Middle:

Without measuring the distance, you can find the middle of a box by crossing lines from the corners (subdivide). This technique of subdivision also works in perspective to find the "perspective center" of a box.

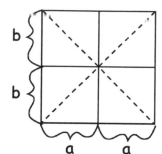

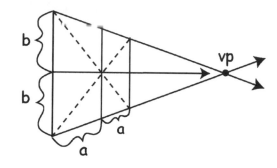

b) Find Equal Distance:

Knowing how to subdivide your box, you can find equal distance in perspective.

1

2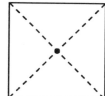

3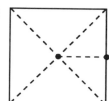

4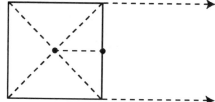

5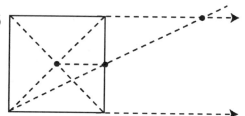

6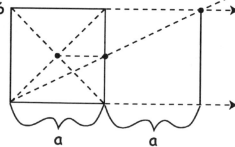

7) you can go on forever with this!

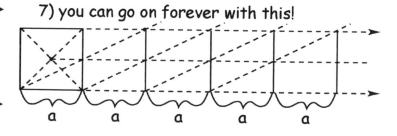

Equal Shapes and Division: More Complicated Division

a) Find the Middle of Each Shape:
Find the next shape of (a) by finding the middle of (b).

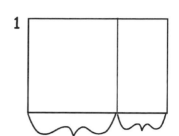

1

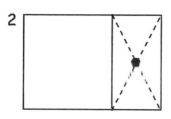

2

b) Find Next Shape:
Find the next shape of (b) by finding the middle of (a).

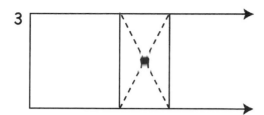

3

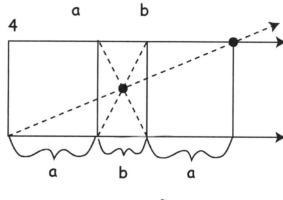

4

a   b   a

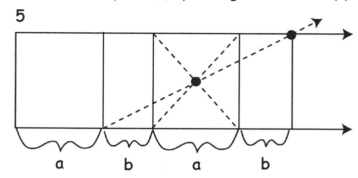

5

a   b   a   b

c) Final Result in Perspective:

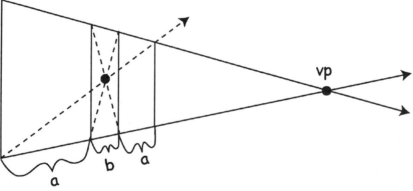

vp

a   b   a

a) To find a shape within a shape:
Find the center of (b), use this as your reference point to find (a) again.

1

b

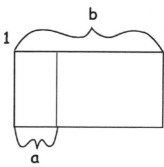

a

2

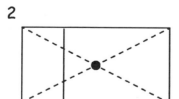

3

a   a

Chapter 4

Trace Points and Vanishing Lines

At any vanishing point you can create a
vanishing line. It is similar in function to a
horizon line, all parallel planes that are also
parallel to the vanishing line will disappear at
the vanishing line. At any point along this
vanishing line you can put a trace point
Trace points are used for angled planes, like
angled rooftops and roads that go uphill or
down hill.

THIS DRAWING IS USING 2 SETS OF VPS; ON
THE HORIZON LINE AND BELOW HORIZON LINE.

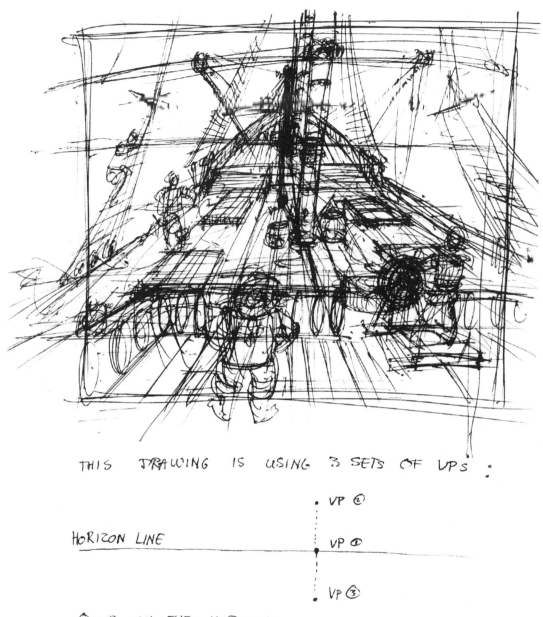

THIS DRAWING IS USING 3 SETS OF VP'S :

. VP ②

HORIZON LINE   VP ①

: VP ③

① VP ON THE HORIZON LINE
② VP ABOVE THE HORIZON LINE A LINE WITH
   THE VP ON THE HORIZON LINE
③ VP UNDER THE HORIZON LINE A LINE WITH
   THE VP ON THE HORIZON LINE .

Chapter 4

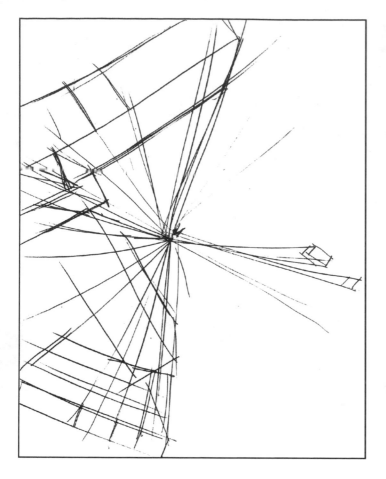

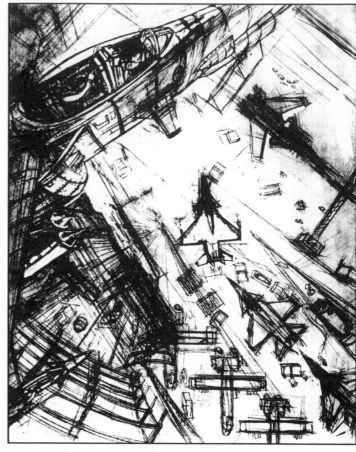

Step by step examples of a drawing in one-point perspective.

Here we've chosen a view looking straight down at the nadir, but all the elements in the drawing are still parallel to our view so they are in one-point perspective.

Sketching out construction lines in the beginning on a separate layer can really help to start visualizing our drawing in perspective.

Keep your drawing, loose but never sloppy in order to have as much creative freedom as possible. The tighter you draw the less freedom you have, and the more you are using the analytical part of your brain. Let go and

feel the drawing. Don't be afraid to make mistakes. Hesitation leads to an unconfident drawing. No matter how correct it is, a fearful and timid drawing can never be as good as a confident drawing, even if the confident drawing is "incorrect".

The more you sketch and the more thumbnails you do, the more authority your drawings will have and the more confident you'll be.

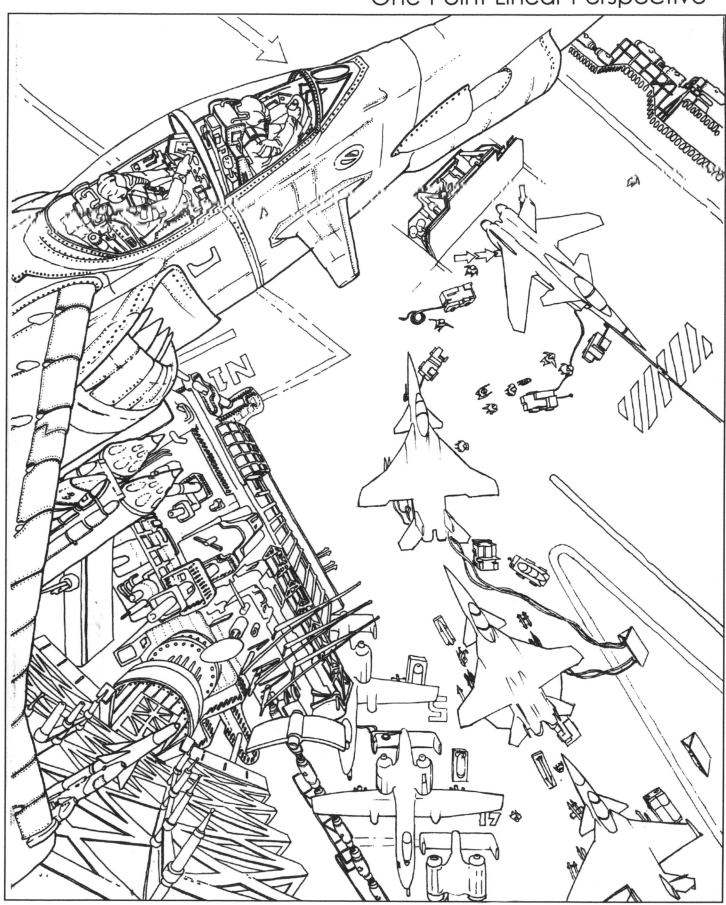

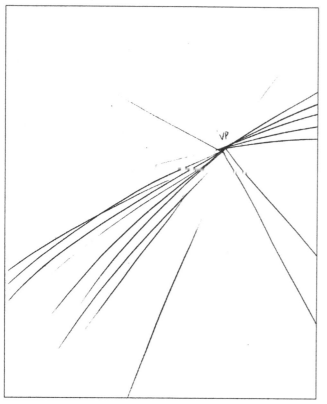

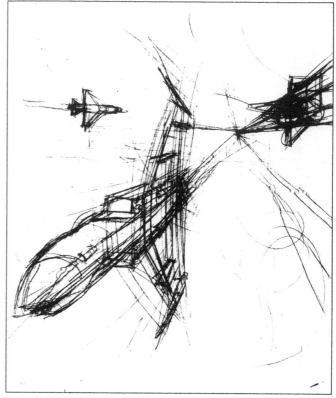

Creative Layout

The Vanishing Point is on the Horizon Line behind the tower

Chapter 4

On the following pages are dozens of thumbnail sketches in one-point perspective. One-point can be a dynamic and simple method to create the illusion of depth correctly as well as helping to create a strong composition.

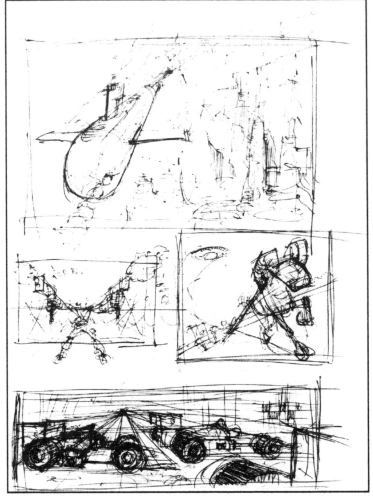

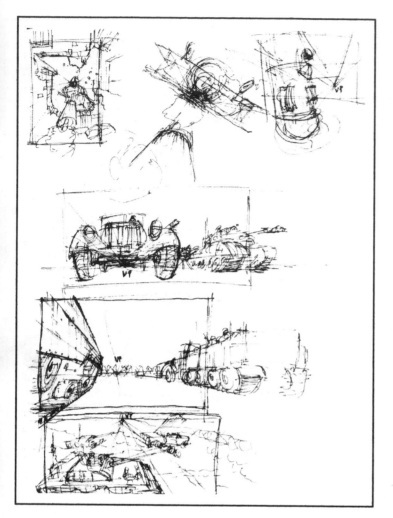

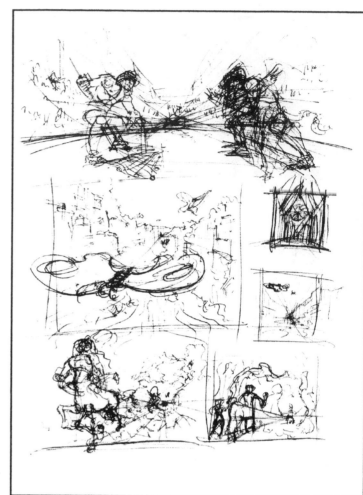

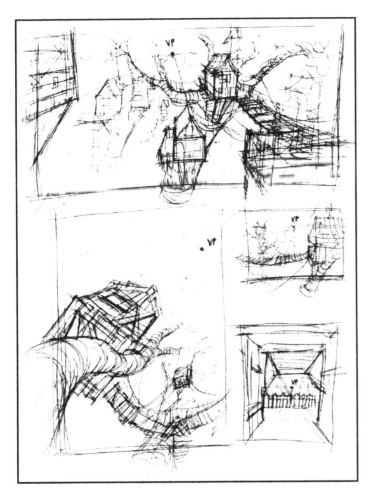

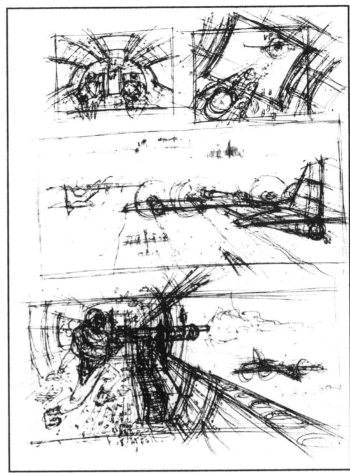

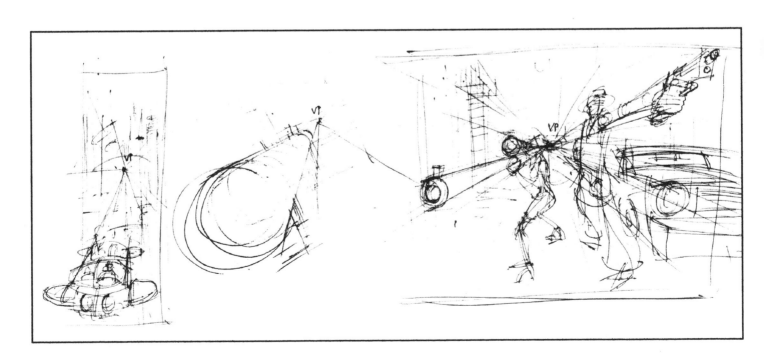

Chapter 4

One Point Perspective Theory

Plan Projection: Pull Down technique Step by Step

a) Gather information:
Plan view (top down view)
Elevation view (side view)
Relationship of station point to object

sp

b) Draw Picture Plane:
The picture plane (pp) can be anywhere, as long as it is in front of you (sp) and perpendicular to the direction you are looking. It is easiest to put the pp touching one side of the plan

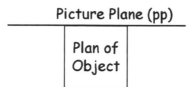

Picture Plane (pp)

| Plan of Object |

sp

c) Draw Horizon Line:
Draw the horizon line (hl) anywhere below the station point (sp) parallel to the picture plane.

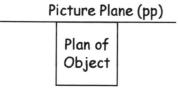

Picture Plane (pp)

| Plan of Object |

sp

Horizon Line (hl)

d) Project Vanishing Point:
Draw a line parallel to the plan, straight up from station point (sp) to the picture plane (pp) and down to horizon line (hl). This is where your vanishing point (vp) is.

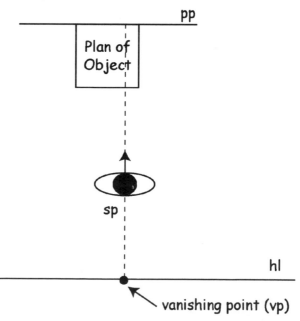

pp

Plan of Object

sp

hl

vanishing point (vp)

One Point Perspective, Plan Projection: Pull Down technique Step by Step

e) Draw Ground Line:
Draw a line below the horizon line (hl) that represents how high your eye level is from the ground, this is your ground line. The distance between hl and gl is h (height).

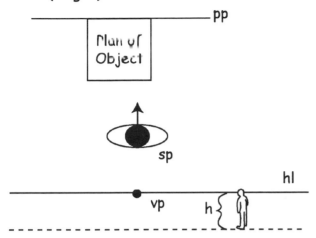

f) Transfer Plan:
Transfer one side of the plan that is on the picture plane (pp) to the ground line (gl).

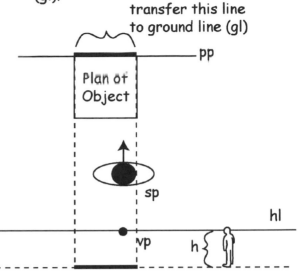

g) Connect Plan:
Connect from vanishing point (vp) to the corners of the line that you just transferred, and continue the lines out.

h) Connect Plan continued:
Connect from station point (sp) to each of the front corners of plan to the picture plane (pp) and straight down until they meet the lines projected from the vanishing point (vp).

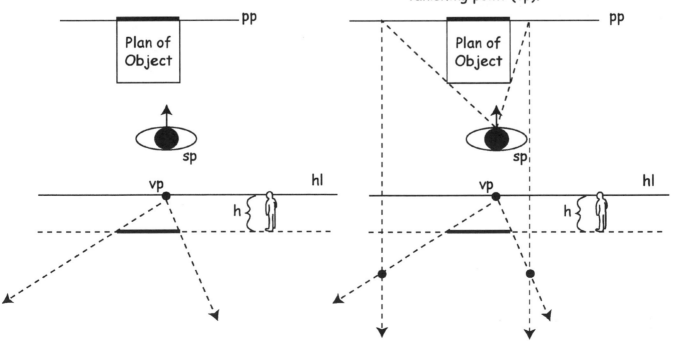

Chapter 4

One Point Perspective, Plan Projection: Pull Down technique Step by Step

i) Connect Plan continued:
Connect a line from the two points you just found (a & b).

j) Connect Plan continued:
Connect all the lines of the plan together.

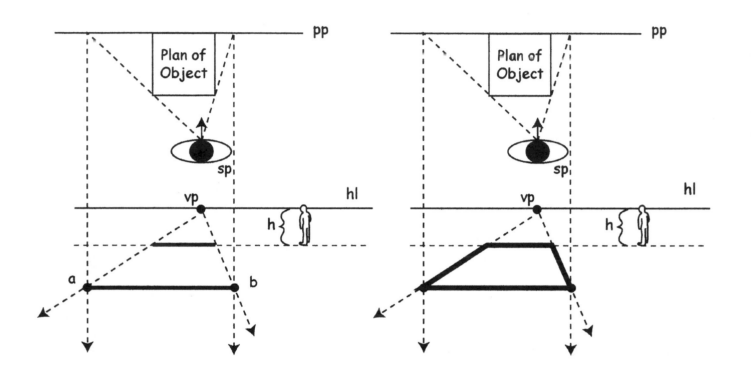

This area represents you (sp) and the plan (object) from above looking down.

This area represents the plan (object) from your (sp) point of view.

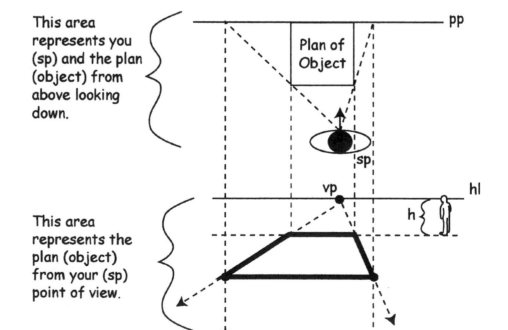

Plan Projection from inside of object

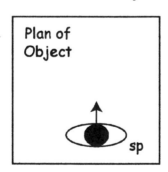

plan projection for an interior: put the sp inside of the plan, and finish without using step i.

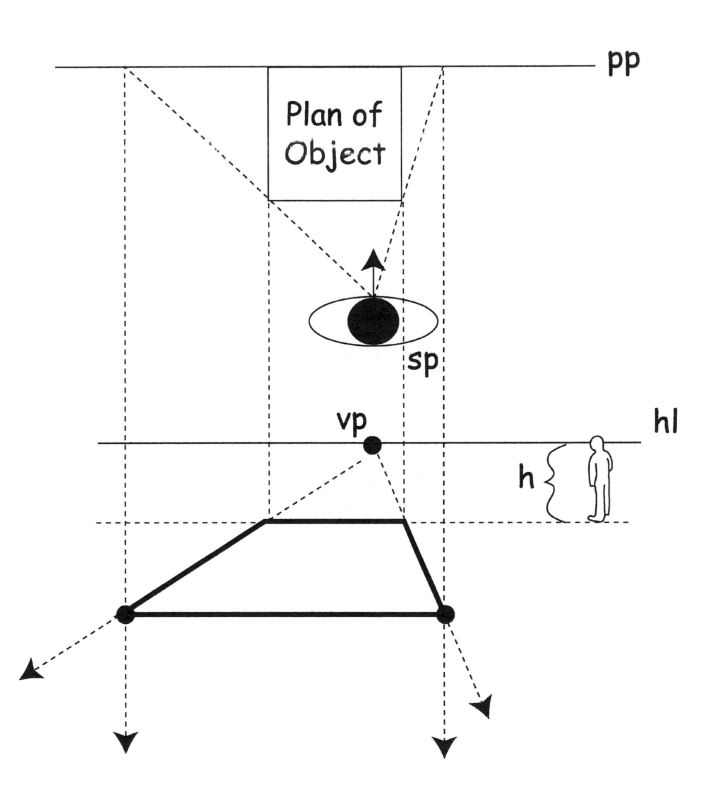

pp

Plan of Object

sp

vp

hl

h

Chapter 5: Two-Point Perspective

The world is Turning...

Two-Point Perspective: Direct Drawing Method

Draw a Horizon Line (hl) and place a center of vision (cv) point on your Horizon line.

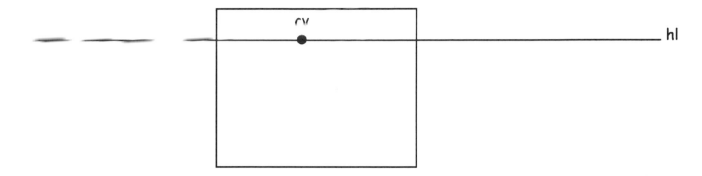

Draw a line straight down from your cv to some point below your drawing, where you end it is your Station Point (sp). Use the 90∞ angle on your triangle from the Station Point, and draw lines out toward the Horizon Line, where they cross the Horizon Line determines your left and right Vanishing Points (vpl & vpr).

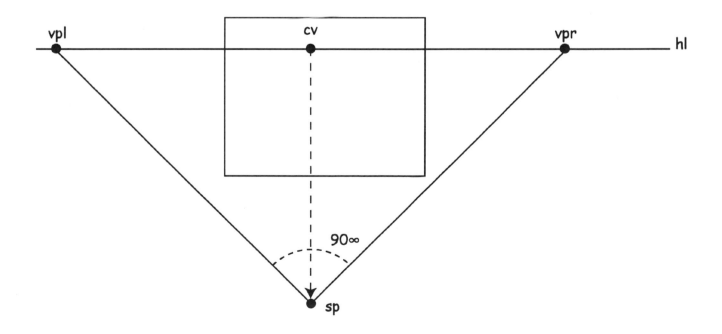

Chapter 5

Two-Point Perspective: Direct Drawing Method

Use the Vanishing Points to create your two-point perspective drawing. All parallel lines will go to their respective vanishing points, vertical lines will remain perfectly parallel.

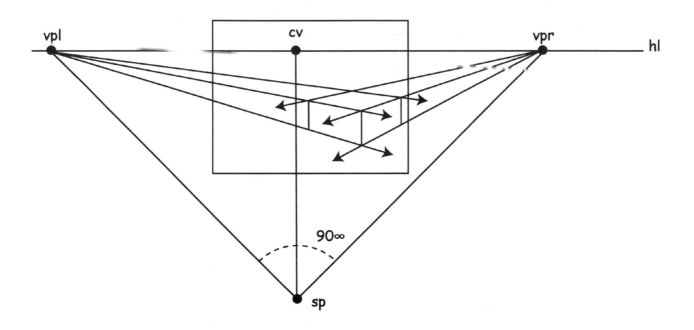

You can use the Center of Vision (cv) as 1pt perspective Vanishing Point (vp).
You can make multiple 2pt perspectives by creating additional sets of vanishing points (vp1 & vp2) as long as they are 90∞ from the Station Point (sp).

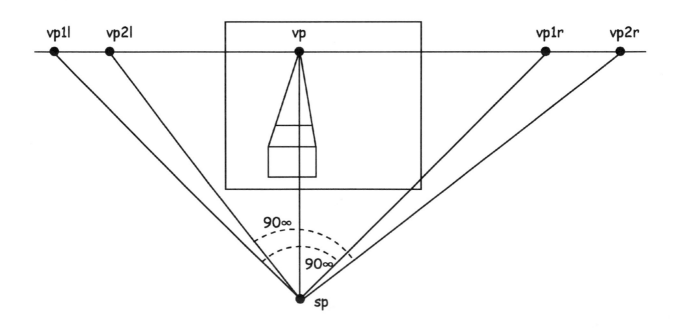

Two-Point Perspective: Direct Drawing Method, Organic

You can use multiple sets of vanishing points, one-point and two-point perspective in drawings of organic shapes, like this canyon, to create convincing perspective.

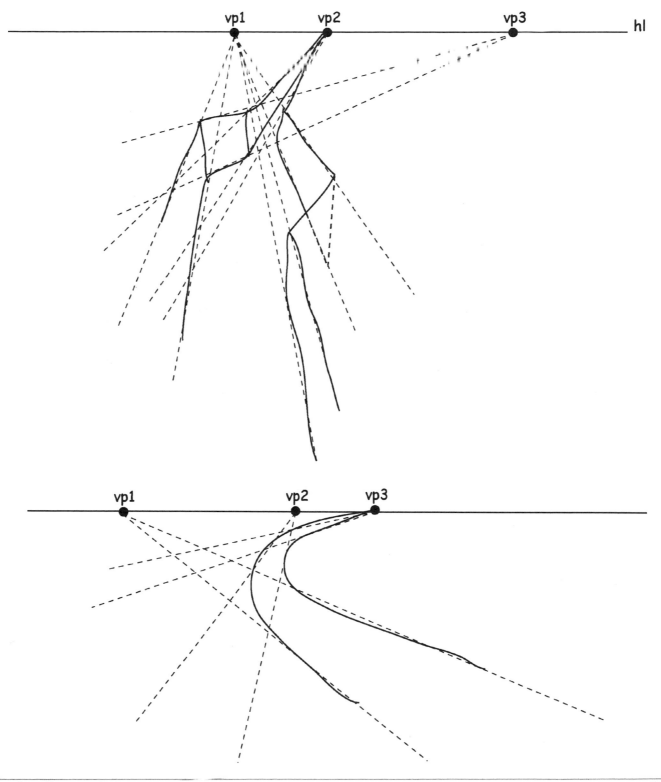

Chapter 5

Two-Point Perspective: Equal Division and Measurement

To measure equal distances in two-point perspective, first create equal distant Measuring Points (mp) from (c), as indicated by (a) and (b) below.

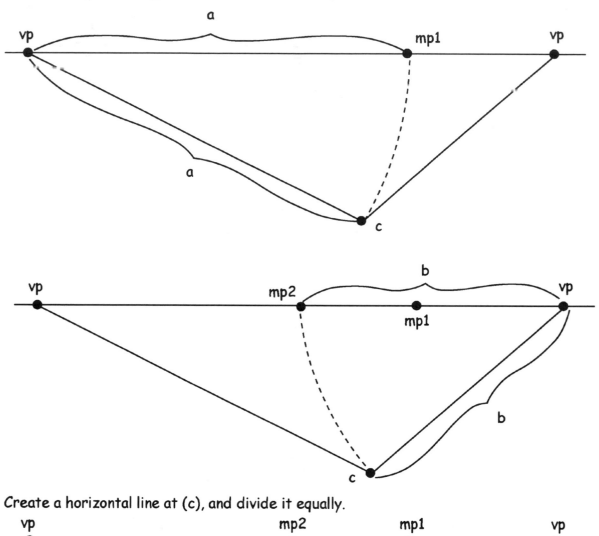

Create a horizontal line at (c), and divide it equally.

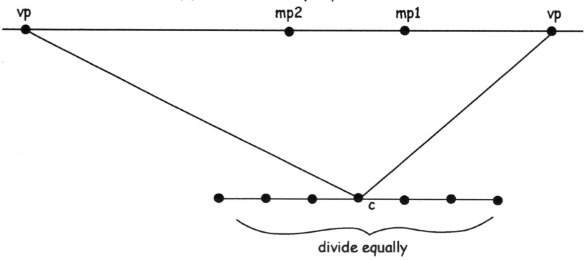

divide equally

Two-Point Perspective: Equal Division and Measurement

Connect points to measuring points, where it crosses projection lines to (vp) are equal measurements in perspective.

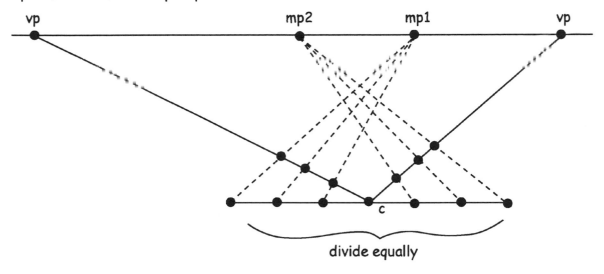

From these equal measurement points, connect lines to vanishing points.

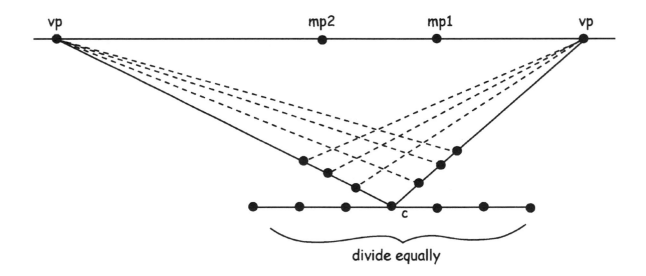

Two-Point Perspective: Equal Division and Measurement

Vertical division is equal to horizontal division.

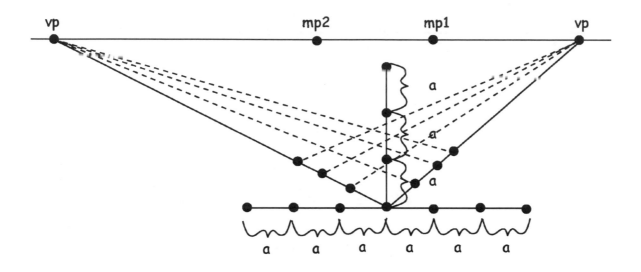

Now all divisions are perfectly equal in perspective.

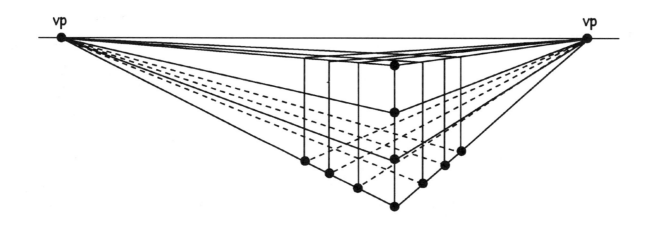

Thumbnail Sketches

Two-point perspective is the most commonly used method to create interesting drawings. It affords considerable flexibility in design while remaining relatively easy to calculate.

You'll note on the following pages these thumbnails put at least one of the vanishing points outside of the picture plane. The most common mistake in drawing two-point perspective is to put the vanishing points too close together thus making the drawing look distorted. By putting your station point far enough below the picture plane you can avoid distortion and have a convincing perspective drawing.

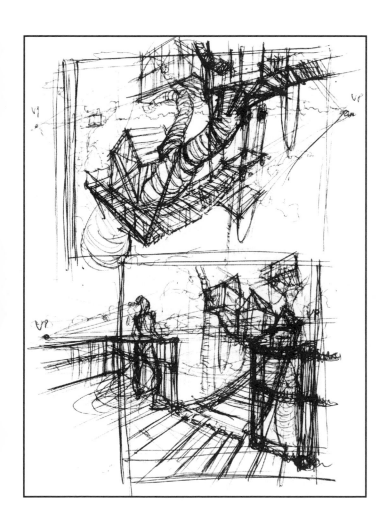

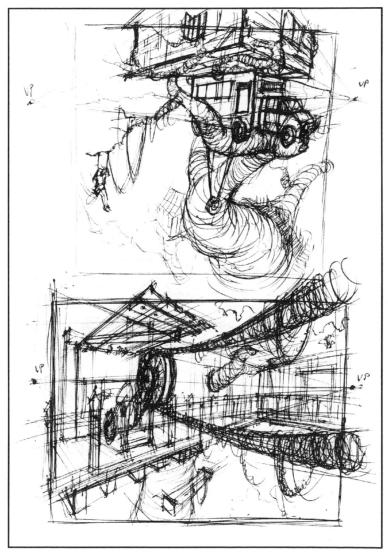

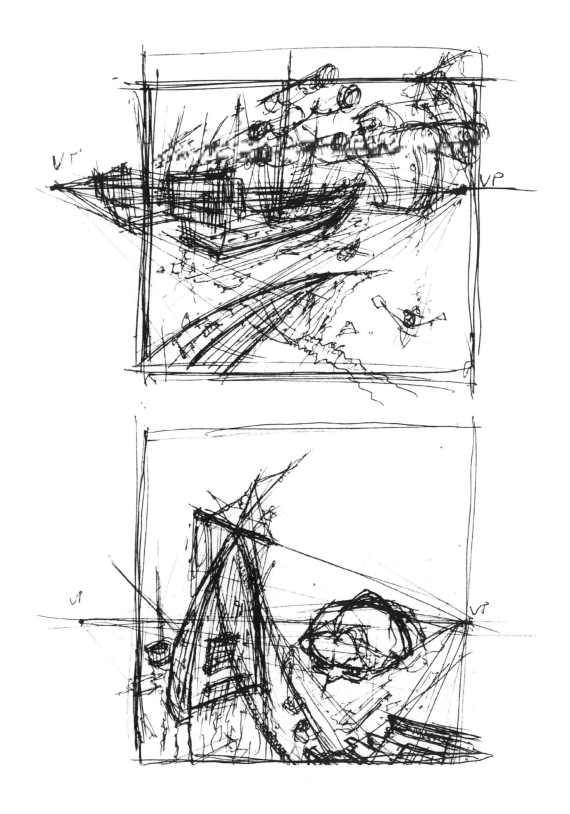

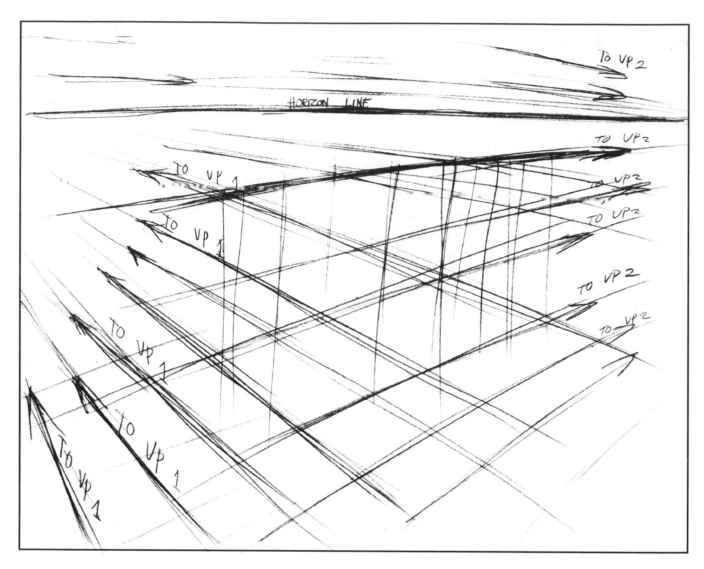

Two-Point Direct Drawing, Step 1- Perspective Grid

On a sheet of tracing paper use the direct drawing method, sketch in construction lines in pencil to aid you in establishing your perspective correctly. These construction lines are also valuable in designing your drawing, helping to create interesting shapes.

This reinforces the principle of perspective that all parallel lines go to the same point on the eye level.

Two-Point Direct Drawing, Step 2 - Block In

Block in your drawings. Be very sketchy at this stage by concerning yourself more with overall composition. If you focus in on the details too soon your design will fall apart, and it will be much harder to finish your drawing.

Work from large shapes to small shapes. The large shapes will help you put the smaller shapes in the correct place. It is much more difficult to work the other way around, if you go for the small shapes and details first they may look great individually, but as a whole will not be unified.

Two-Point Direct Drawing, Step 3 - Refine

After you've worked out your composition you can start refining your drawing. Clean up the lines and add more details. We are still working in pencil and on layers of tracing paper at this stage to keep our drawing clean so we don't want to put in too many details. Save that energy for the final, inked drawing. This refined drawing is too be a clear, strong layout that we can use to help us finish the drawing with confidence.

Two-Point Direct Drawing, Step 4 - Finish
Ink your refined drawing. We like to use vellum or fine layout paper, not tracing paper for the final drawing. You can now apply atmospheric perspective to your line quality.

Chapter 5

Get used to do a lot of
thumbnails before you go
to the finished drawing.
Work out different concepts and find
out solutions for problems you may
find at this stage.

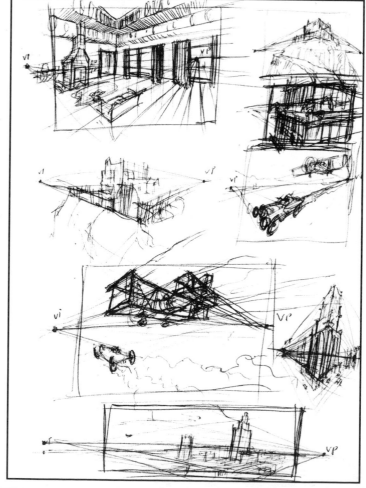

One of the advantages in doing
thumbnails is that at this size, you can
plot the vanishing points really far
apart.

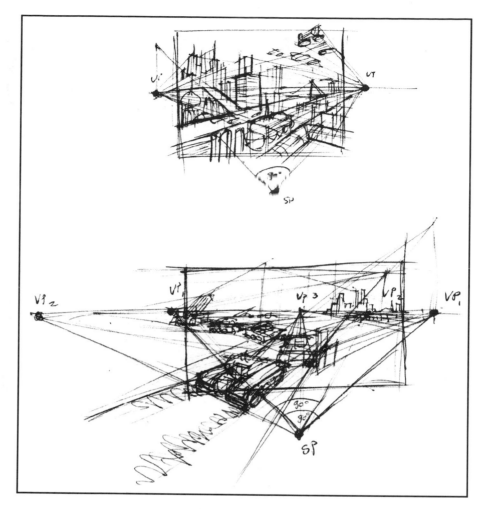

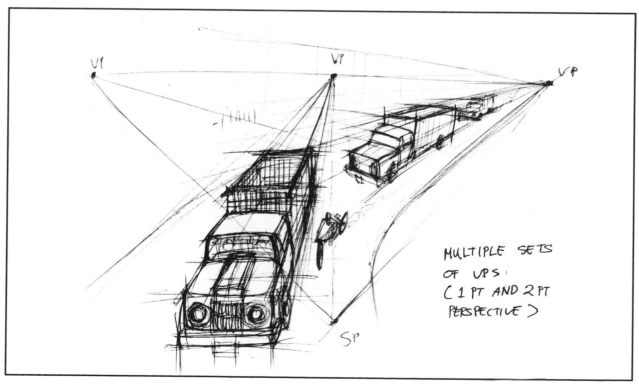

MULTIPLE SETS
OF VPS
(1 PT AND 2 PT
PERSPECTIVE)

Chapter 5

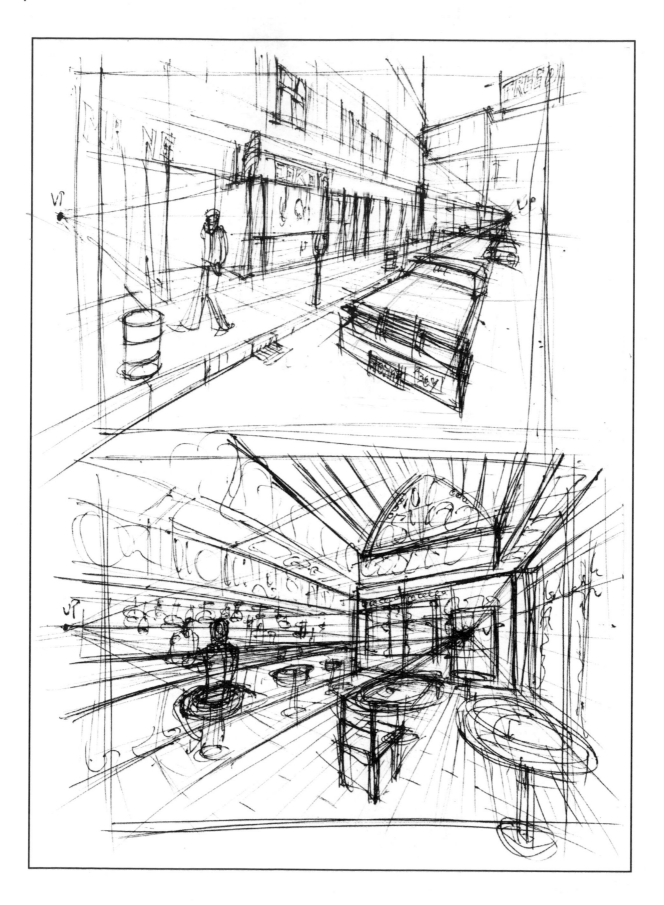

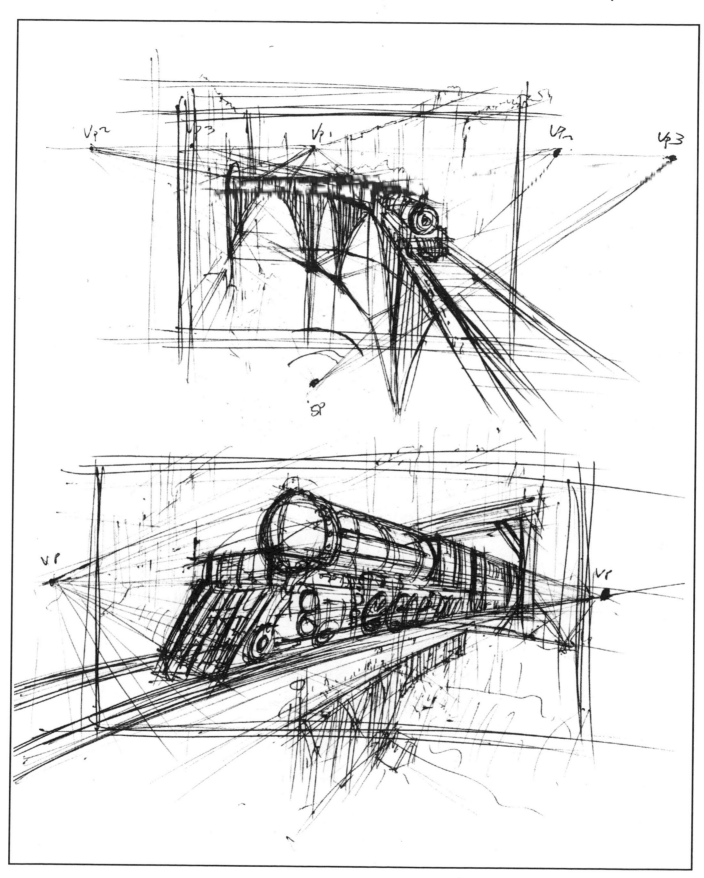

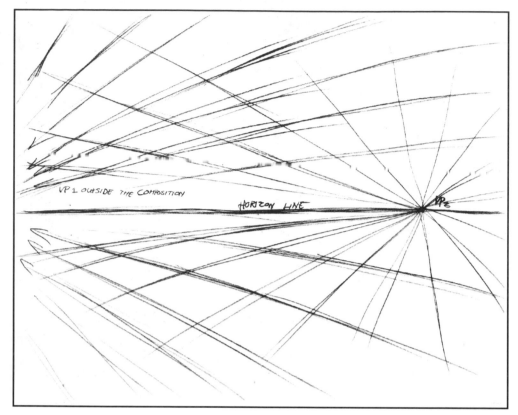

It is acceptable to put one of the vanishing points inside the composition, as long as it is not so much to the middle of the composition.

Notice that the right side area of the drawing, near the vanishing point is slightly distorted. This is acceptable because the distortion area does not cover a large space.

The distortion on the right side of the composition, in some ways actually enhances the overall feeling of the gigantic space.

Although It is not always mandatory to start a composition from the method of building construction lines and it's respective vanishing points (like a rough sketch for example), the artist should at least be aware of the approximate location of the vanishing points.

Two-Point Perspective Theory: Pulldown Technique

Plan

Center of Vision: (cv) the
point your eye is looking at.

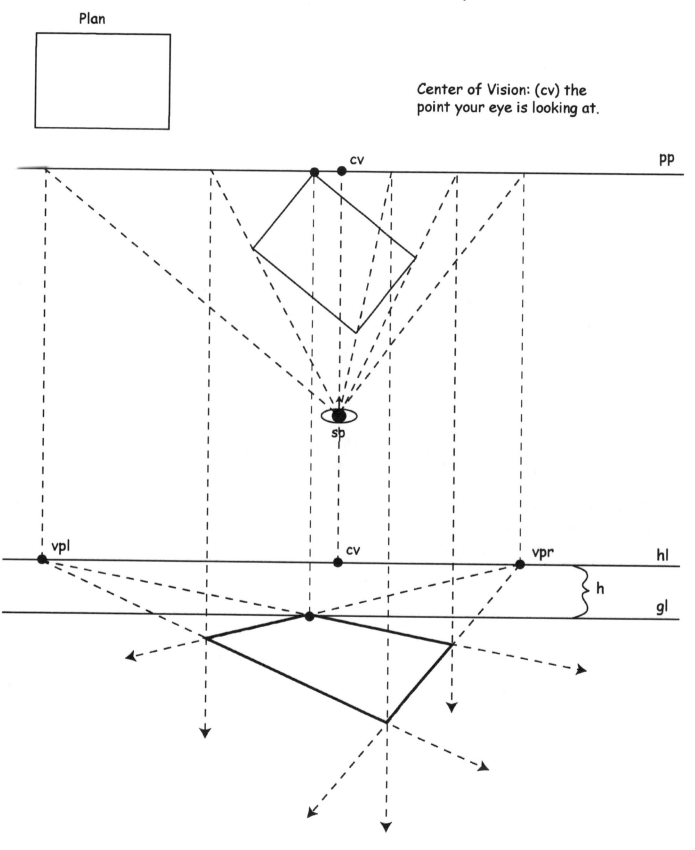

pp

cv

sp

vpl

cv

vpr

hl

h

gl

The world shed in light...

Light and Shadow in Linear Perspective

One-Point and Two-Point Light and Shadow

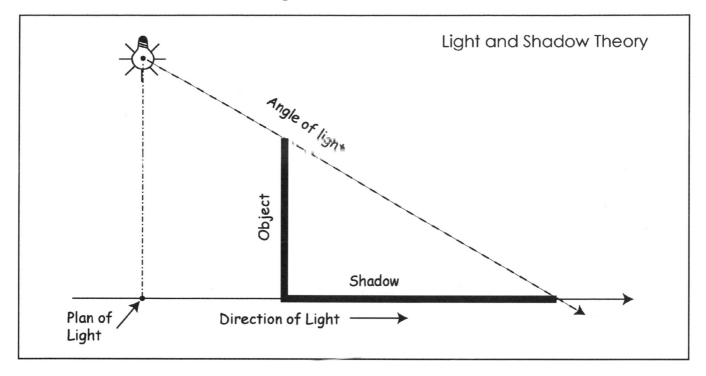

Light and Shadow Theory

Angle of light

Object

Shadow

Plan of Light

Direction of Light ⟶

One-Point, Two-point Sun Light

Plotting sunlight in one-point & two-point perspective is divided into three approaches, depending on the direction of the sun.

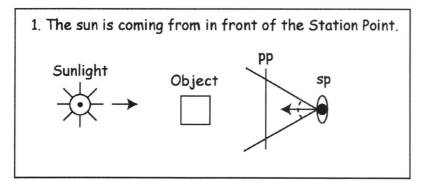

1. The sun is coming from in front of the Station Point.

Sunlight   Object   pp   sp

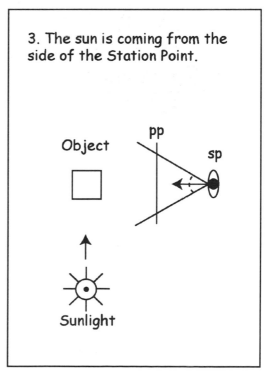

3. The sun is coming from the side of the Station Point.

Object   pp   sp

Sunlight

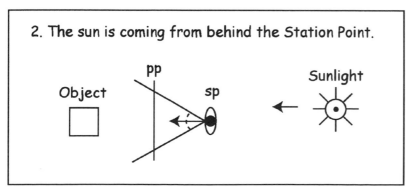

2. The sun is coming from behind the Station Point.

pp   sp

Object   Sunlight

Chapter 6

One-Point and Two-Point Light and Shadow: Local Light

Calculation for local light in one-point and two-point
perspective is identical to calculation of light in
isometric perspective.

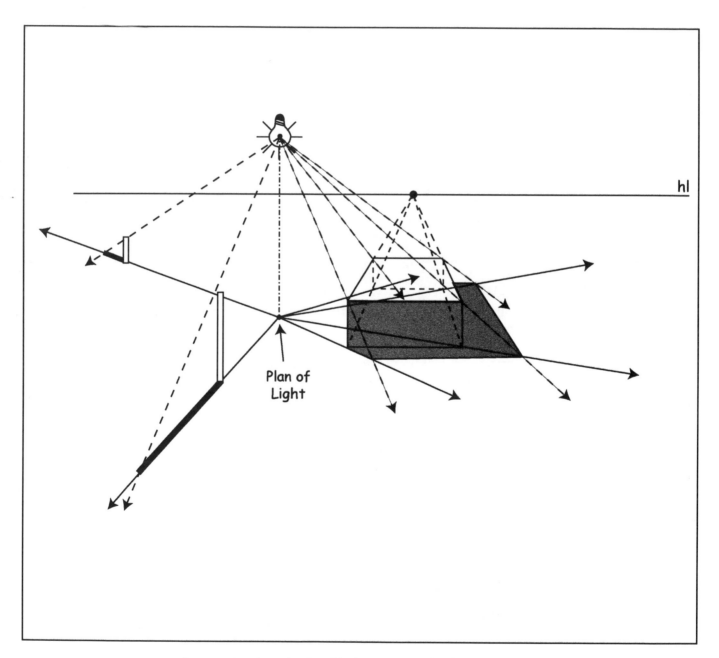

Determine how high off the ground the light
source is. Project direction of light from Plan of
Light, project Angle of Light from light source.

One-Point and Two-Point Light and Shadow: Sunlight from side

The direction of the sunlight is always parallel to the Horizon Line, when the sun is 90∞ to the side of the Station Point.

In one-point perspective when the sunlight (direction of light) is coming from 90∞ to the side of the Station Point, the drawing needs three groups of values: Dark for the cast shadow value group, Light for the light value group and gray 50% for the halftone, or oblique value group.

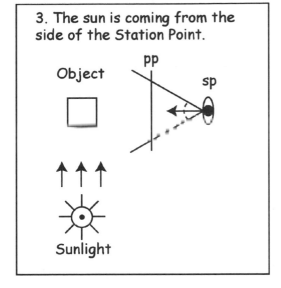

3. The sun is coming from the side of the Station Point.

Object

pp

sp

Sunlight

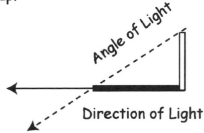

Angle of Light

Direction of Light

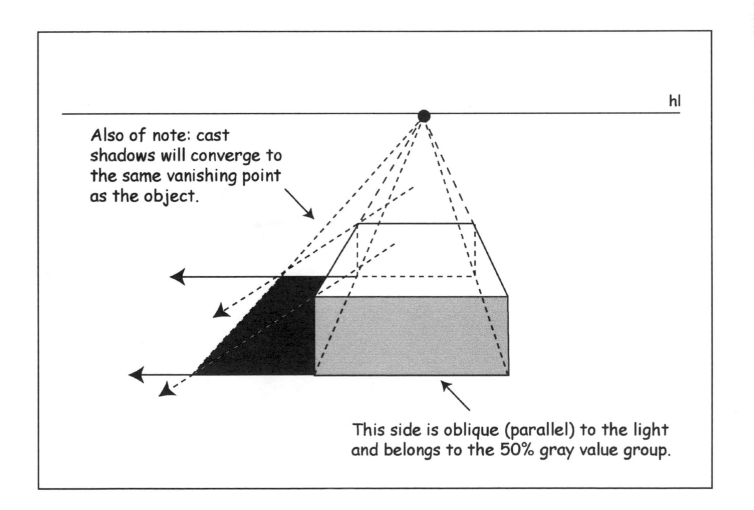

hl

Also of note: cast shadows will converge to the same vanishing point as the object.

This side is oblique (parallel) to the light and belongs to the 50% gray value group.

Chapter 6

One-Point and Two-Point Light and Shadow: Sunlight from front

Because the sun is so far away, it is theoretically at an infinite distance. Certainly too far for us to calculate! So we consider the Earth to be a flat plane, and use the Horizon Line as the distance of the sun.

1. The sun is coming from in front of the Station Point.

Sunlight   Object   pp   sp

Sky

Horizon Line (hl)

Plan of Sun   Earth

The closer the sun is to the Horizon Line, the longer cast shadows will be. Just as during Sunrise and Sunset cast shadows are longer.

Angle of Light

Direction of Light

hl

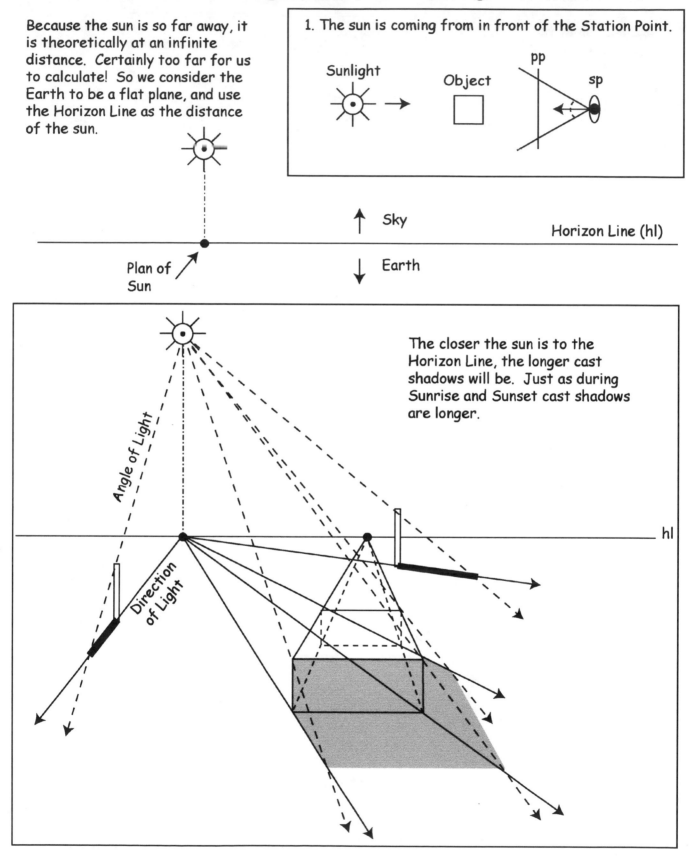

Light and Shadow in Linear Perspective

One-Point and Two-Point Light and Shadow: Sunlight from behind

When the sun is behind, you cannot see where the sun is coming from , but you can see where your shadow is going.

Every shadow in sunlight is **parallel** to each other. You can determine the direction of the sunlight (which is the same as the direction of the shadow) by only knowing the direction of shadow on one object.

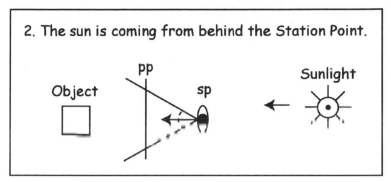

2. The sun is coming from behind the Station Point.

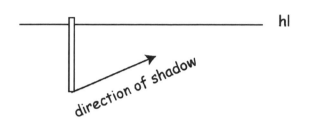

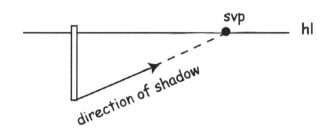

Where the direction of the shadow for a particlar object (in this case a vertical line on the ground) meets the Horizon Line (hl), is where the Shadow Vanishing Point (svp) for the shadow is located.

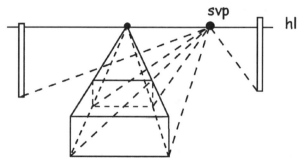

All cast shadows in that environment will go to that one Shadow Vanishing Point (since all cast shadows are parallel).

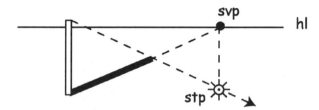

Where the shadow ends on a particular object, determines where the representation of the sun, or Sunlight Trace Point (stp) is. Draw a line from the top of the object through the end of the shadow, where it crosses a vertical line straight down from the (svp) is where the (stp) is.

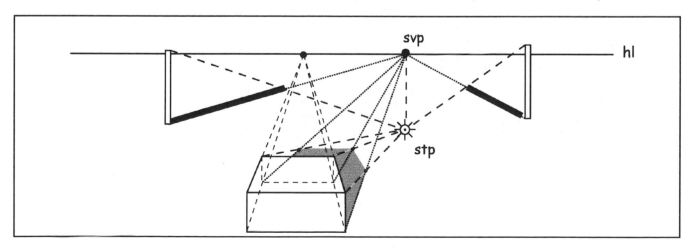

Light source: local light from the foreground on the right, outside of the composition.

Light source: local light from the foreground, outside of the composition.

Light source: sunlight appears inside the composition, on the left side (Sunlight on the background).

Light source: sunlight appears inside the composition, on the left side, close to the middle (sunlight on the background).

Light source: local light from the middle ground.

Light source: sunlight from the background (left).

Light source: sun/ moon light from the left side.

Light source: moon light from the right side.

There should be no difference between the value pattern and composition of the thumbnail, and the finished drawing. The only difference is the amount of detail in the finished work, which should be more than the thumbnail.

Sensitivity is another thing that the artist should apply to the finished drawing.

Light source: local light from the middle ground.

Light source: Sunlight / moonlight from the background (at the end of the tunnel on the right).

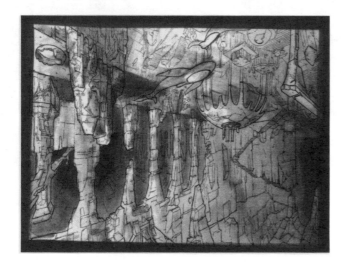

Light source: sunlight from the background (at the end of the tunnel on the left).

Light source: sunlight from behind the viewers on the right side.

Step by step light and shadow

After choosing the thumbnails that you want to develop to the finished drawing, determine the position of the light source.

Draw the vanishing lines from the plan of the light source to every vertical lines or planes that are touching the horizontal planes. Put these vanishing lines on the horizontal planes, which are the surface of the water and some parts of the ceiling of the cave. In the case of the sunlight, the light/ shadow vanishing point is on the horizon line below the sun.

Block the form shadows and the cast shadows with the same value.

Incorporate the local tone of the water.

Last step:

Incorporate atmospheric perspective and smoothen the transitional tones.

Look back at the thumbnail you choose and compare the value patterns with the finished one, they should look pretty similar.

Chapter 6

Light source: sunlight straight from the right, in 45 degree angle.

Light source: sunlight straight from the left, in 45 degree angle.

Light source: sunlight straight from the left, in 45 degree angle.

Light source: sunset.

*

*

Light source: sunlight from the background.

Light source: local light from the foreground (the gun).

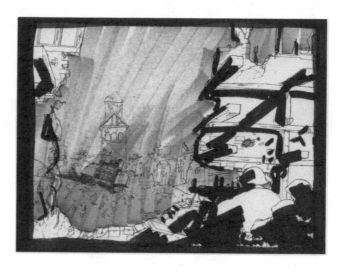

Light source: sunlight from the right in 45 degree angle.

Light source: sunlight from the right in 45 degree angle.

Imagine that the wall is actually without the big hole in the middle. The plan of the light (shadow VP) is actually the target sight. So the vanishing lines on the wall are coming from the the target sight and spread out. The cast shadows on the wall are from the lines or planes that comes out from the wall (from the middle vanishing point) and follow the direction of the vanishing lines. The light source itself is close to the face of the gunner. The light on the tip of the gun barrel is not affecting the cast shadows on the wall. It is not affecting the wall because that light is actually outside the building (imagine the broken wall as one solid square cropping of the tip of the gun).

For the sun that is coming from the background, all vertical planes the artist face are in shadow (form shadows). The only major cast shadow is on the ground, coming from the plan of the church tower and spread out. This spread out cast shadow is using the angle that coming from light/ shadow VP on the horizon line underneath the sun.

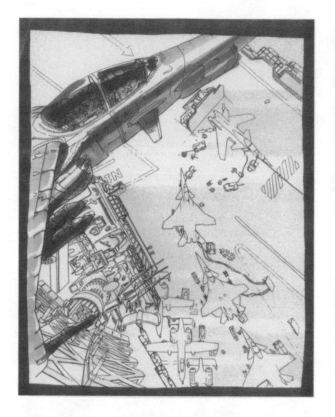

Although the calculation of the light and shadow is important, the artist should think about the overall value to enhance the composition.

Chapter 6

Sunlight

Creative Layout

Local light

This is the only thumbnail that the light source is behind the viewer.

Light and Shadow in Linear Perspective

Incorporate atmospheric perspective to both the thumbnails and the finished composition.

Chapter 6

These are value thumbnails and finished works.

Sometimes it is not necessary to do the line drawing first before the finished drawing. As long as the artist think about the overall value, shape and the composition.

Creative Layout

But it's always true that drawing thumbnails are necessary before the artist goes into the finished composition.

Creative Layout

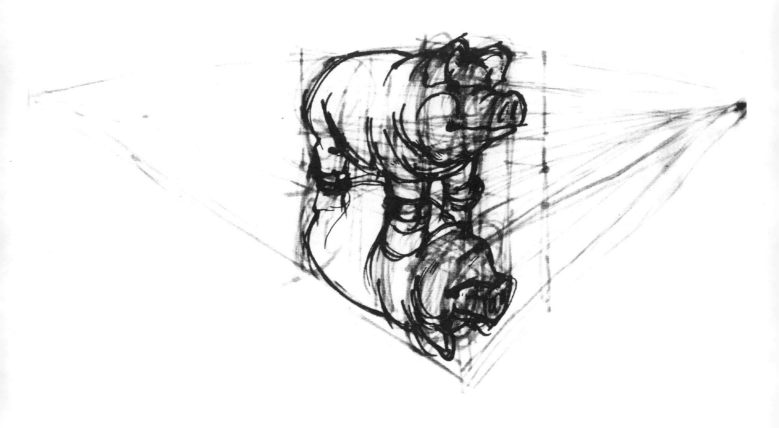

The world in a mirror...

Creative Layout

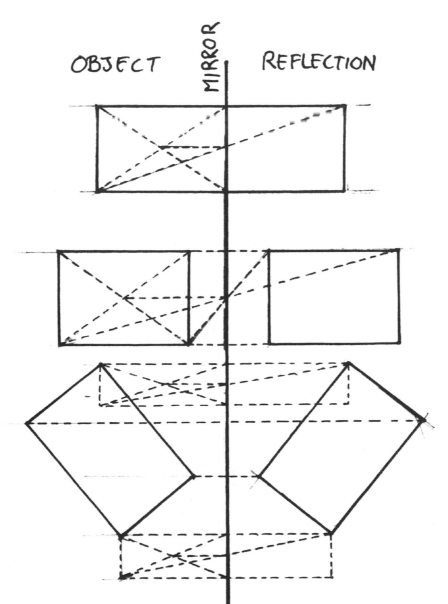

OBJECT   MIRROR   REFLECTION

① GROUND REFLECTION
② 1 pt. OBJECT AND 1 pt. MIRROR
③ 2 pt. OBJECT AND 2 pt. MIRROR
④ 2 pt. OBJECT AND 1 pt. MIRROR
⑤ 1 pt. OBJECT AND 2 pt. MIRROR
         OR
2 pt. OBJECT AND 2 pt. MIRROR
WITH DIFFERENT SET OF VPs

THERE ARE MORE THAN 5 TYPES OF REFLECTION FOR 1 pt. AND 2 pt. PERSPECTIVE.

WE JUST DON'T WANT TO DRIVE YOU GUYS **INSANE**.

ASK YOUR TEACHER IF YOU WANT TO KNOW MORE.

Chapter 7

Ground reflection

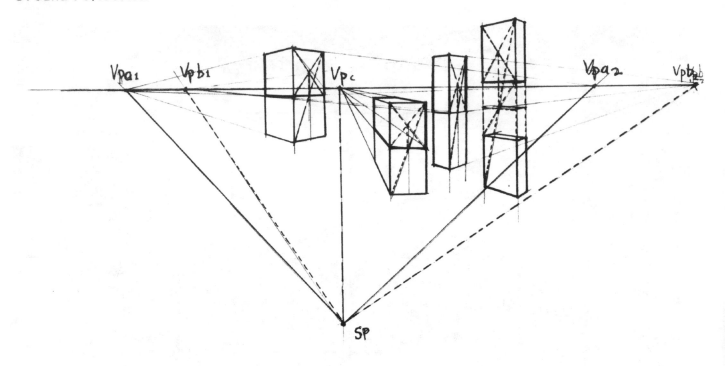

One point object one point mirror

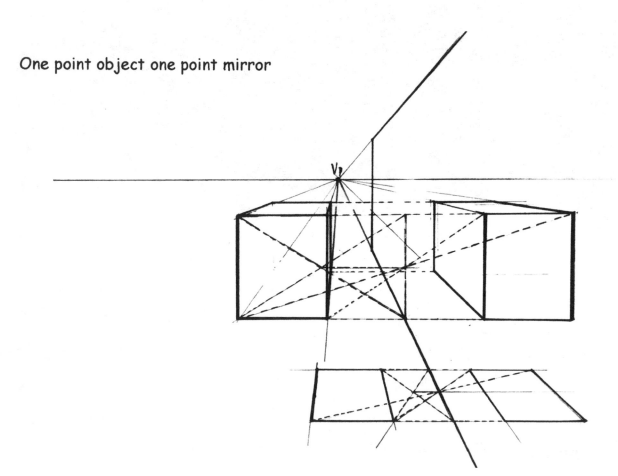

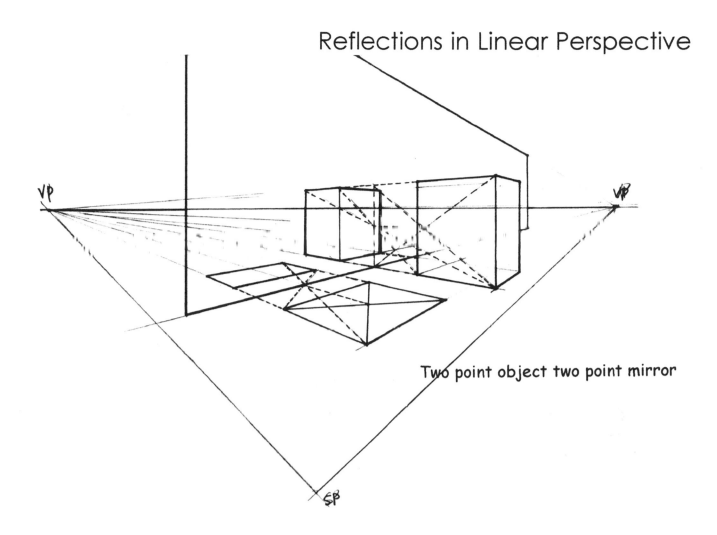

Two point object two point mirror

Two point object one point mirror

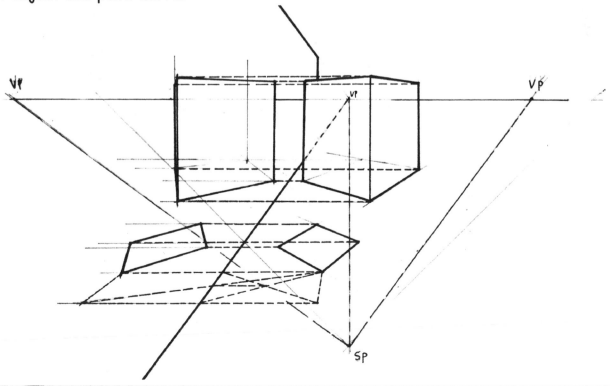

Chapter 7

Another two point object one
point mirror

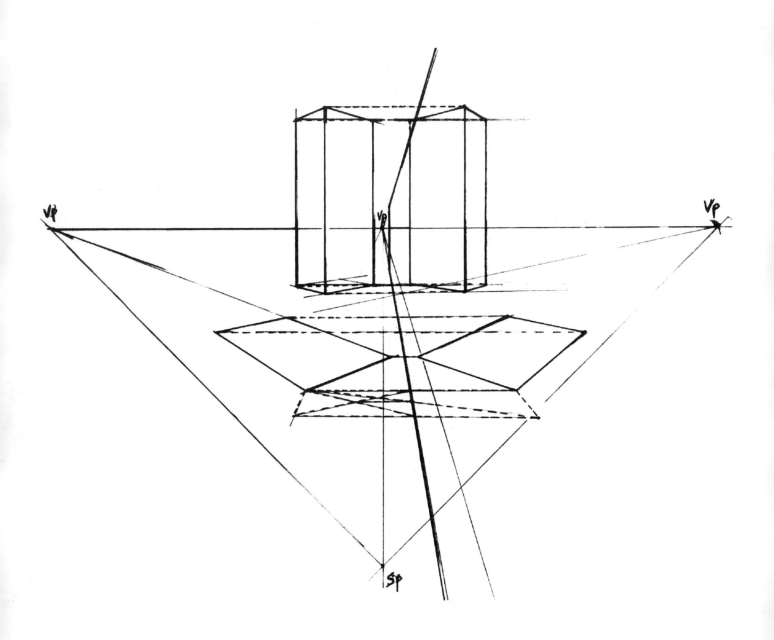

One point object two point mirror

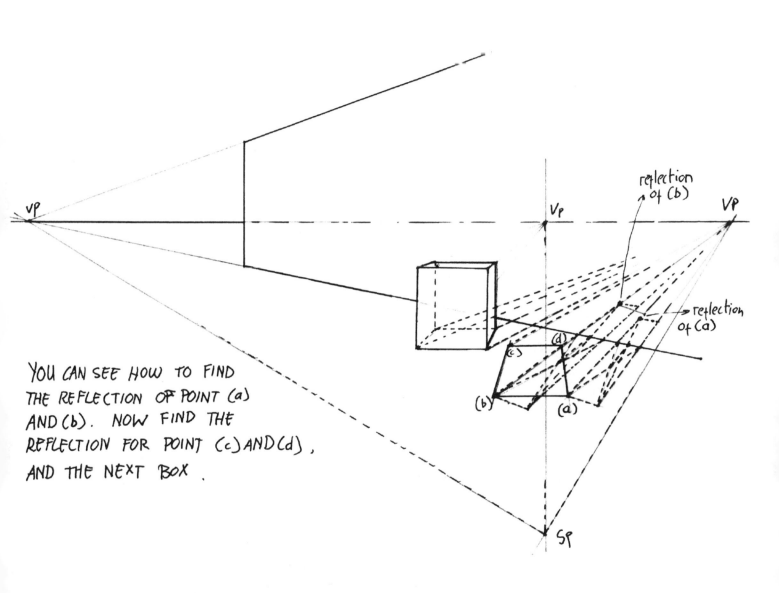

VP

VP

VP

reflection of (b)

reflection of (a)

(d)

(c)

(b)

(a)

SP

YOU CAN SEE HOW TO FIND
THE REFLECTION OF POINT (a)
AND (b). NOW FIND THE
REFLECTION FOR POINT (c) AND (d),
AND THE NEXT BOX.

It is not necessary to draw
the plan of the object first
in order to draw the object.
Nevertheless the artist
should know where it is in
order to draw the
reflection.

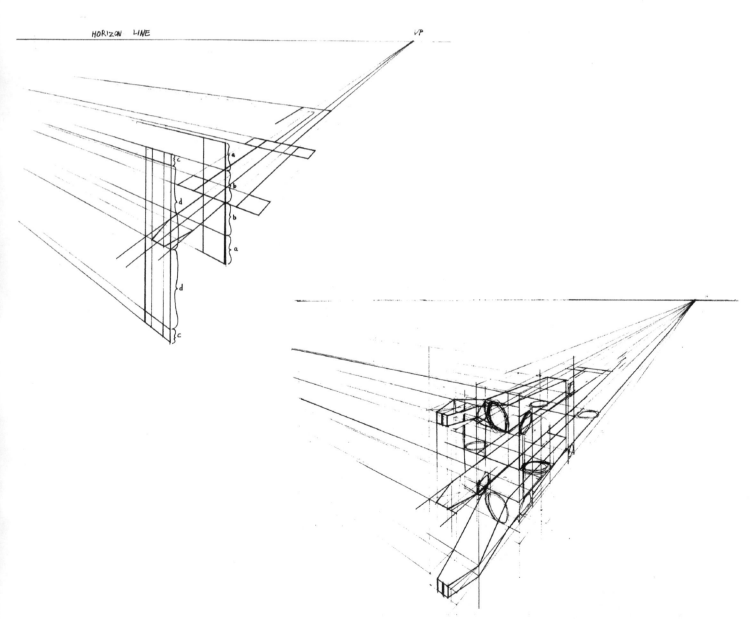

Chapter 7

In two dimensional work (drawing and painting) the object and the reflection should never-ever be identical in shape. The most common mistake for artists when drawing the reflection of an object is to flip the same object (upside down or side way, depends on the mirror location) to convey the reflection.
The only time that the artist can do this is when the object is far away from the viewer(for ground reflection; when the plan of the object close to the horizon line).

As you can notice in this drawing, we can see the top of the shoulders and leg of the princess, but on her reflection we see the underneath of her chin and her dress/robe.
The reflection in this case is basically a 'looking up' view of the princess.

Creative Layout

Chapter 8: Two-Point Vertical

The world up and down...

Creative Layout

Two-Point Vertical Linear Perspective

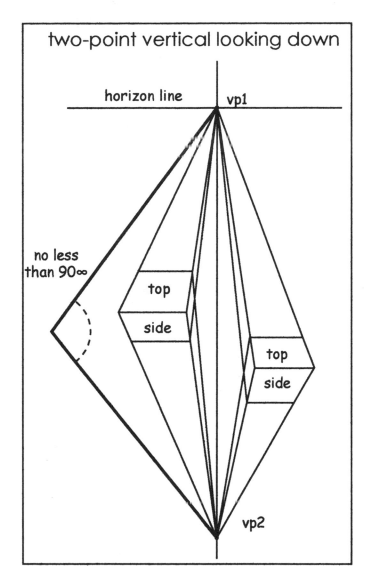

two-point vertical looking down

horizon line — vp1

no less than 90∞

top

side

top

side

vp2

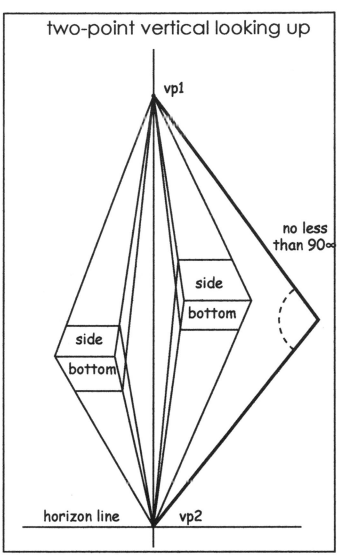

two-point vertical looking up

vp1

no less than 90∞

side

bottom

side

bottom

horizon line — vp2

To put it in simple words, two-point vertical is basically a regular two point perspective that goes sideways. It contains similar rules to regular two point perspective, like having both or at least one of the vanishing points outside the composition. Moreover, it should not have less than 90 degree angle on the left and right sides of the objects. The difference is that the horizon line in two point vertical is only on one of the vanishing points. And in two point vertical the viewer is either looking down or looking up at the objects, depends on where the artist puts the horizon line.

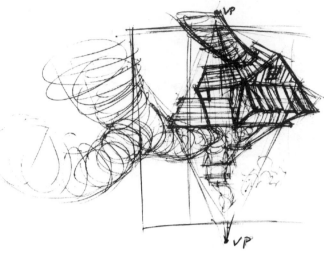

Although in two point vertical the vanishing point and the horizon line are outside the composition, the artist should be aware of where they are.

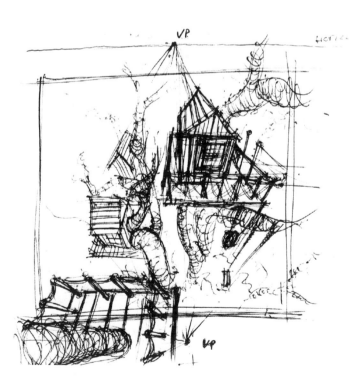

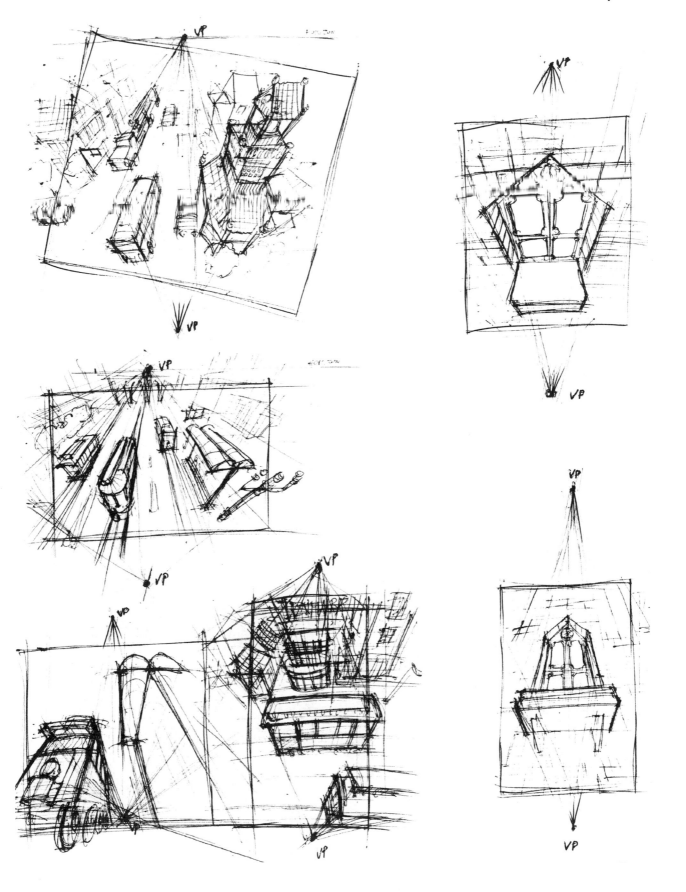

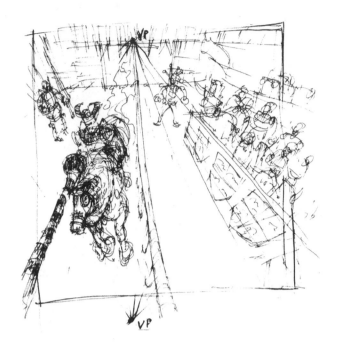

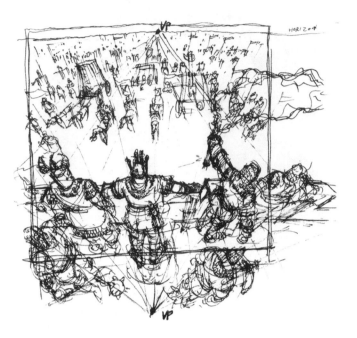

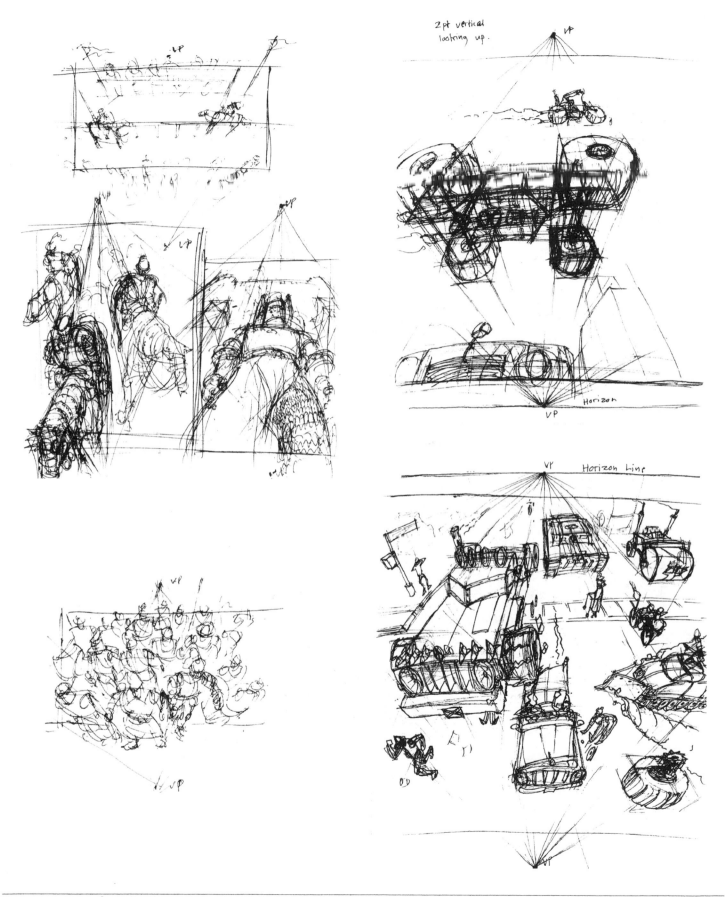

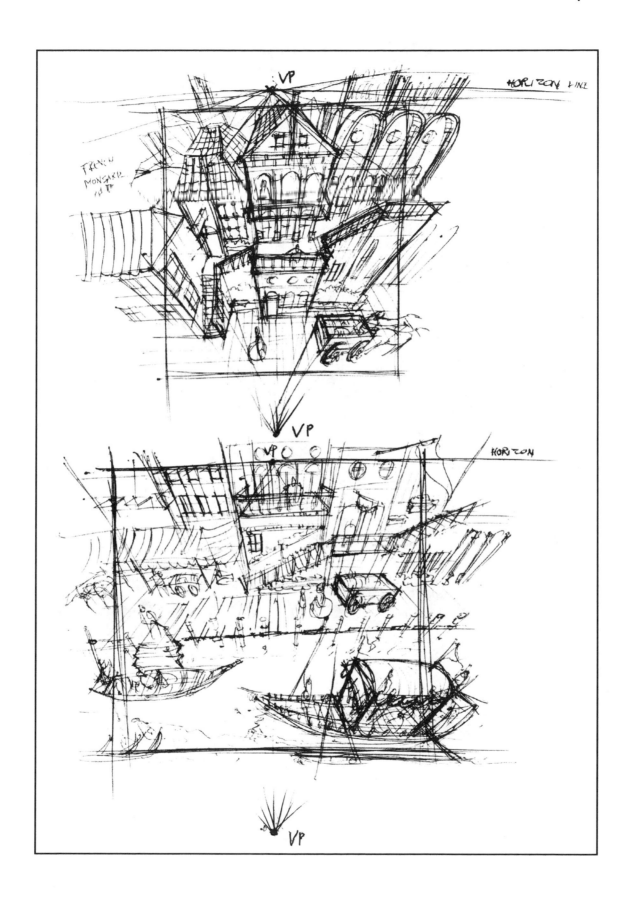

Creative Layout

Chapter 8

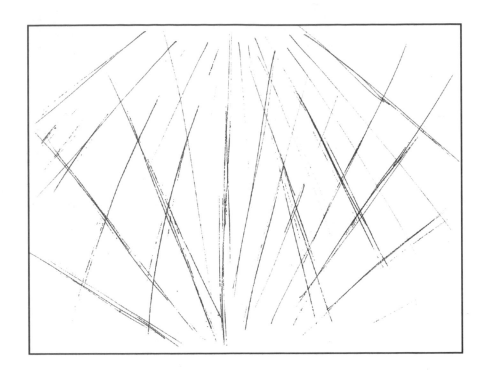

Step by step two point vertical

Creative Layout

Sometimes, if you run into drawing mistakes, you don't have to redraw everything, just cut and paste a piece of paper on the section of the composition that needs to be changed and redraw only that specific section.

Refine it a little more...

In the finished line drawing, the small boat on the bottom of the left hand corner was replaced by the oar of the front boat. This makes a better composition (circular composition) than the rough drawing.

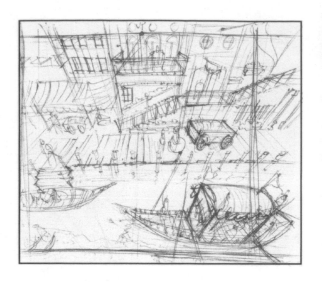

Use calculation of cast shadows to make the drawing correct, but not at the expense of the composition.

Chapter 9: Three-Point Linear Perspective

The world in a triangle...

One set of three point perspective

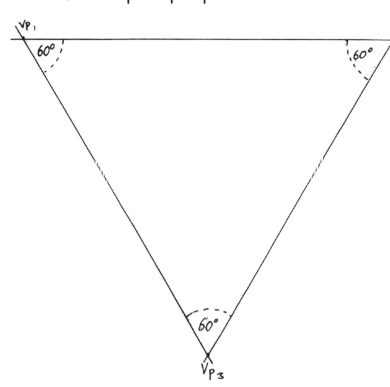

Make an equilateral triangle: the distance from each each vanishing points are the same. Which makes the angle of each vanishing point 60 degree.

Draw the object using the three vanishing point.

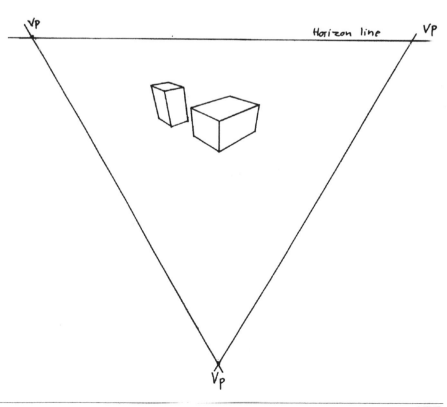

Chapter 9

Three point perspective and two point vertical

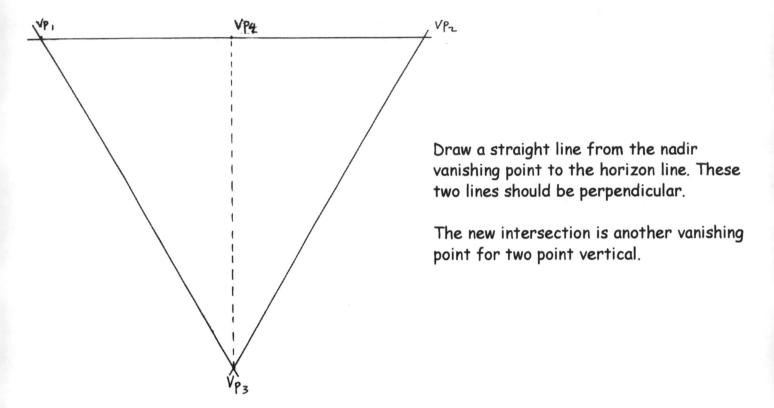

Draw a straight line from the nadir vanishing point to the horizon line. These two lines should be perpendicular.

The new intersection is another vanishing point for two point vertical.

Draw the object using either two point vertical or three point perspective. All of the objects are using the same vanishing point in the nadir

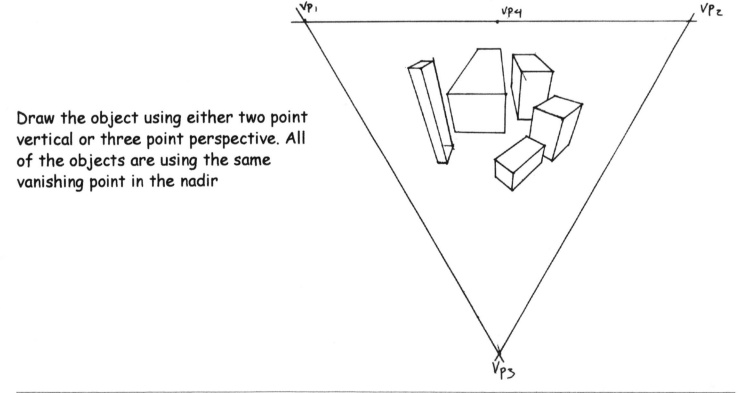

Multiple sets of three point perspectives and two point vertical

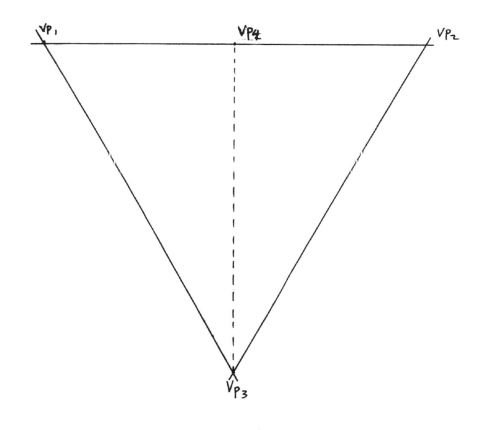

Find the station point by:
a. take the same distance from the left or right vanishing point to the middle vanishing point at the horizon line.
b. put this distance from the the middle vanishing point on the horizon line to the direction of the nadir vanishing point.

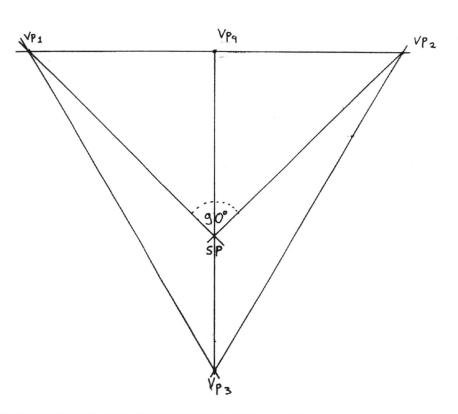

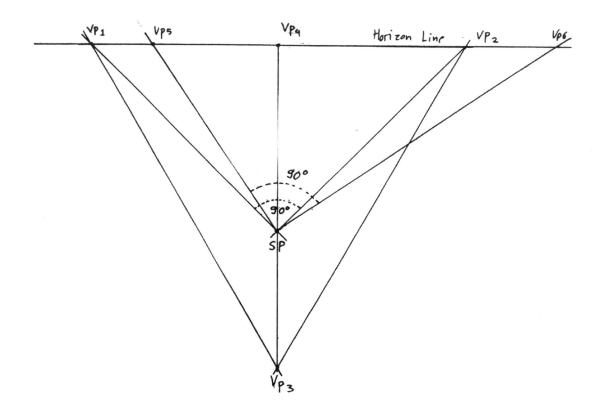

As long as the angle of the two vanishing points on the horizon line is 90 degree on the station point, the artist can make as many sets of vanishing point as he or she like.

Creative Layout

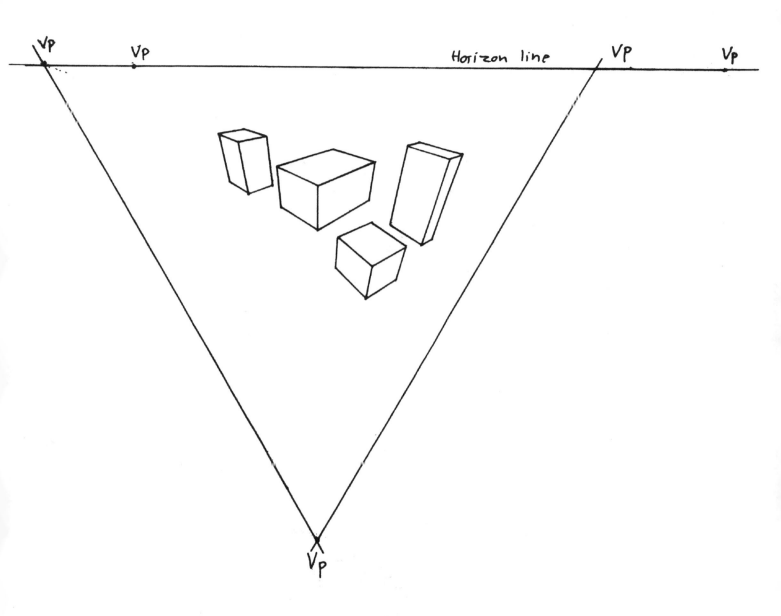

All of these objects are sharing the same nadir vanishing point.

Chapter 9
Three point thumbnails

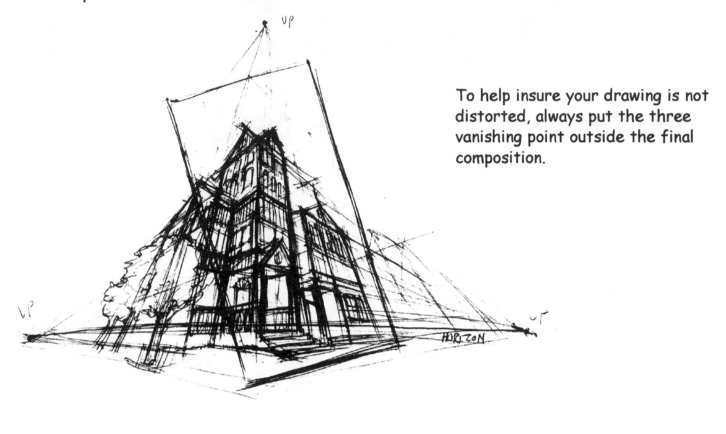

To help insure your drawing is not distorted, always put the three vanishing point outside the final composition.

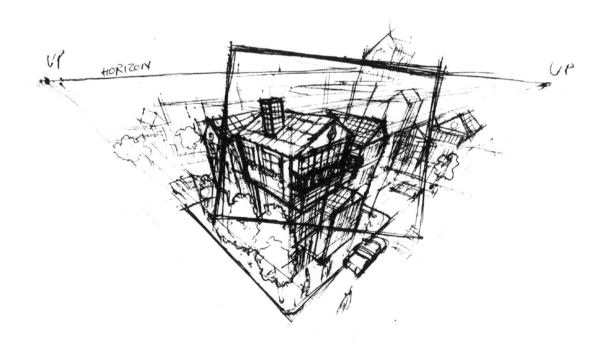

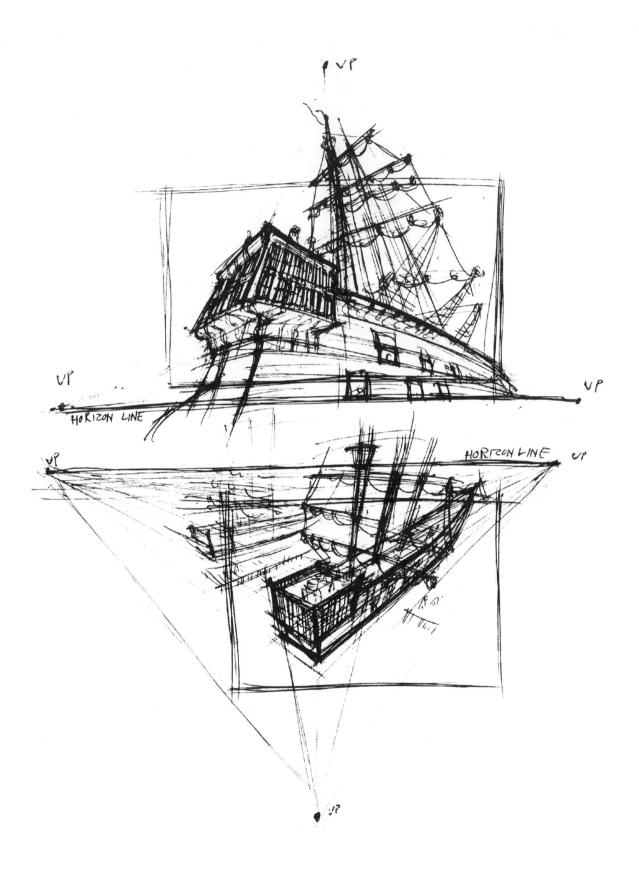

Three-Point Linear Perspective

These thumbnails combined three point perspective and two point vertical.

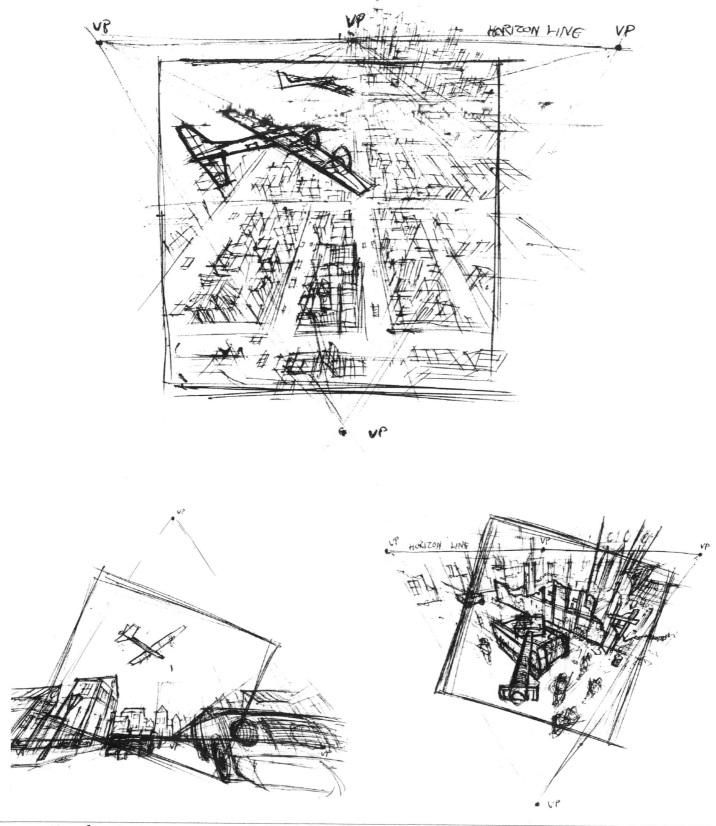

In these two drawings (left and right page), the artist uses two point vertical for the treasure chests, but ignores the correct way of using two point vertical and three point perspective for the characters. This was done consciously in order not to show any distortion on the characters anatomy (except for the distortion that comes from the using of the zenith vanishing point for the left drawing and the nadir vanishing point for the right drawing).

Zenith: top/up

Nadir: bottom/down

Chapter 10: Fish-Eye

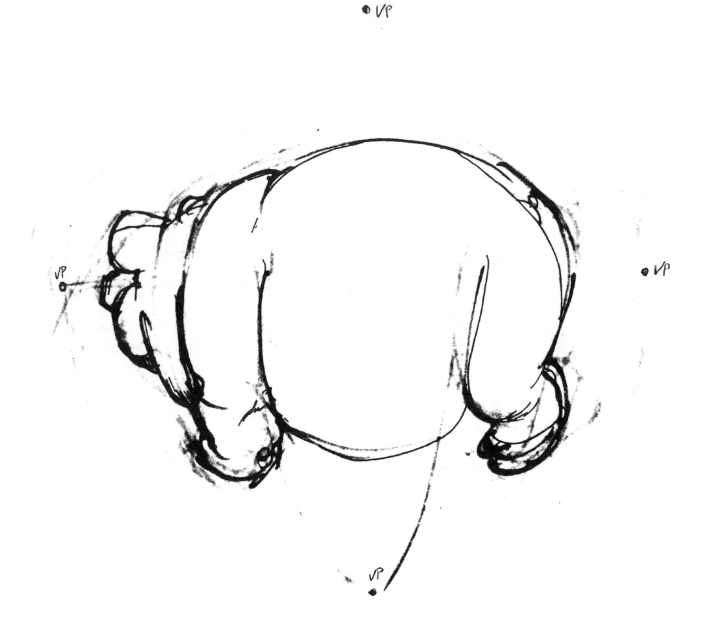

Everything in the world at once...

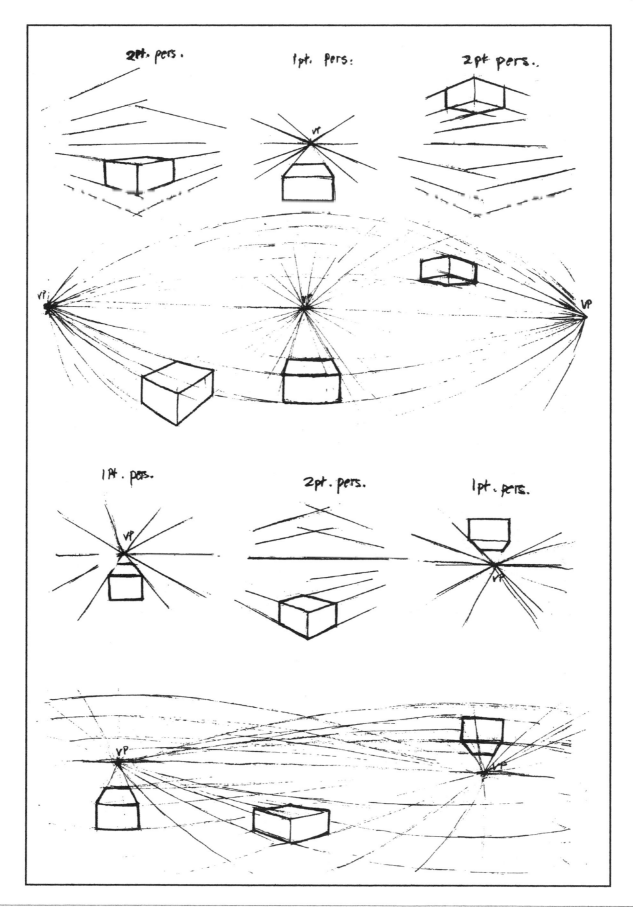

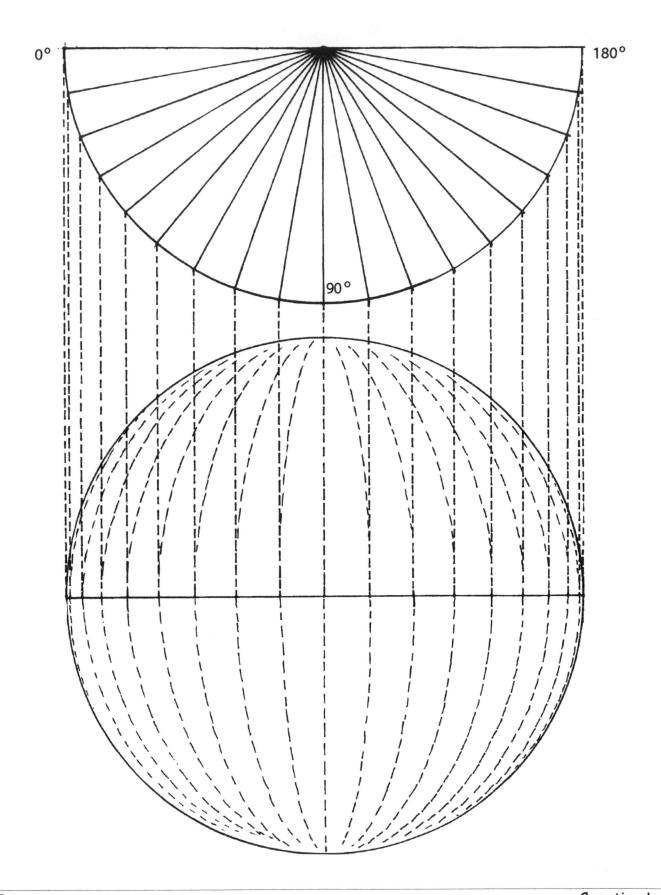

Fish-Eye Grid - Five Point

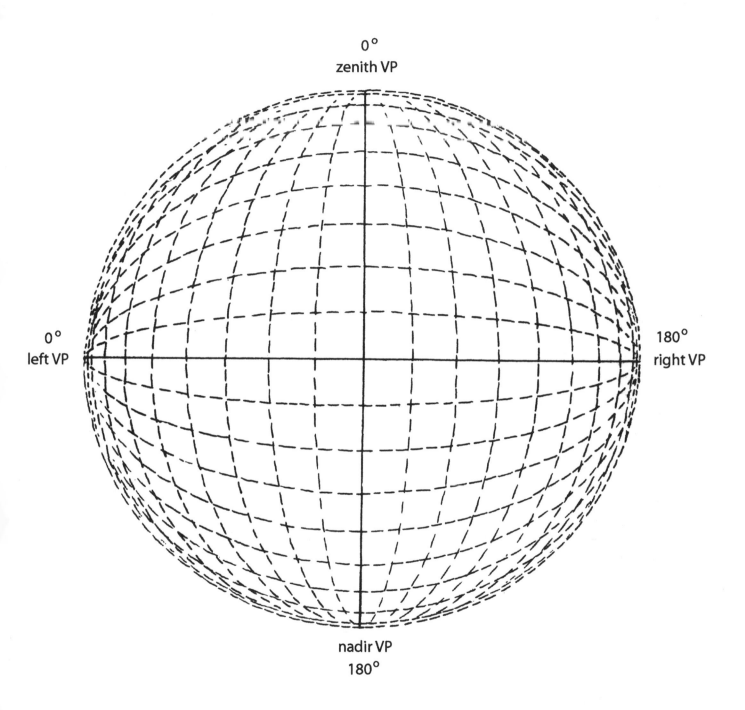

Use this grid as a foundation for your Fish-Eye drawing, make a enlarged photocopy of the grid and work on top of it with a sheet of tracing paper. You can also make the grid free hand. As you will see in the next few examples, we don't necessary have to use the entire circle when we do a Fish-Eye composition, you can use half of the circle or even a quarter of a circle.

Chapter 10

The artist can use the middle Vp as the vanishing point on the horizon line (eye level composition) or the middle VP as the nadir vanishing point (looking down composition).

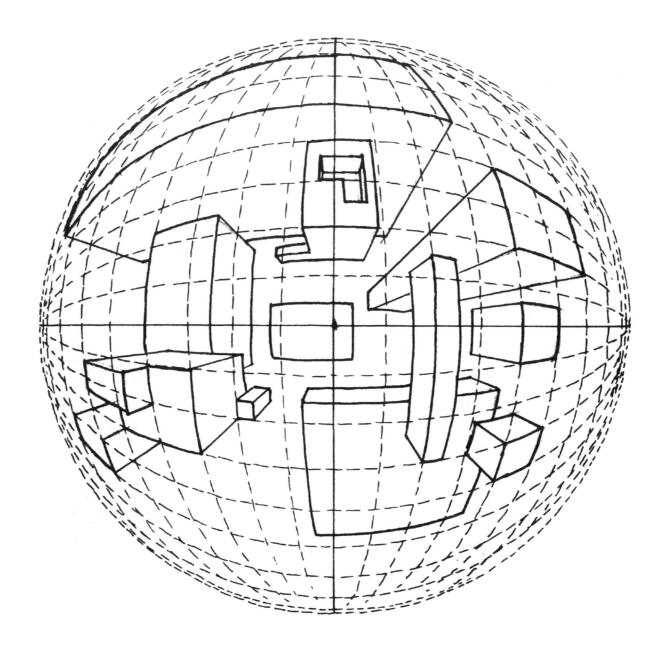

When using 5point Fish-Eye, the vanishing lines that comes from the middle VP are always straight and constant, while the vanishing lines coming from the top, bottom, left and right Vps are always curved, connecting from one Vp to the other on the same axis.

In this example, the VP in the middle is the nadir vanishing point.

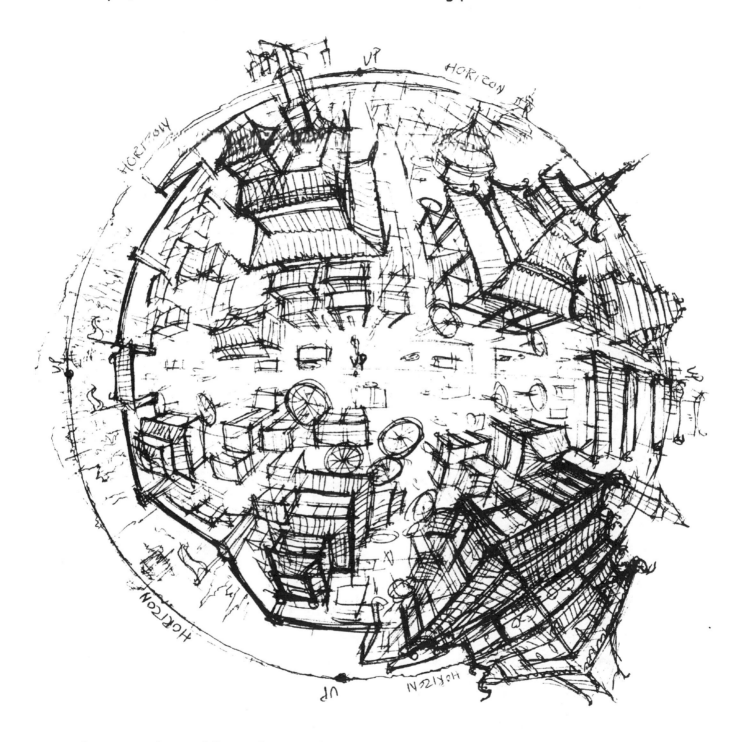

Because the VP in the middle is the vanishing point of the nadir, than the line that makes the whole cyrcle (the farthest line from the middle) is the horizon line.

In this page, the middle horizontal line is the Horizon line. Also, they are all using only half of the circle.

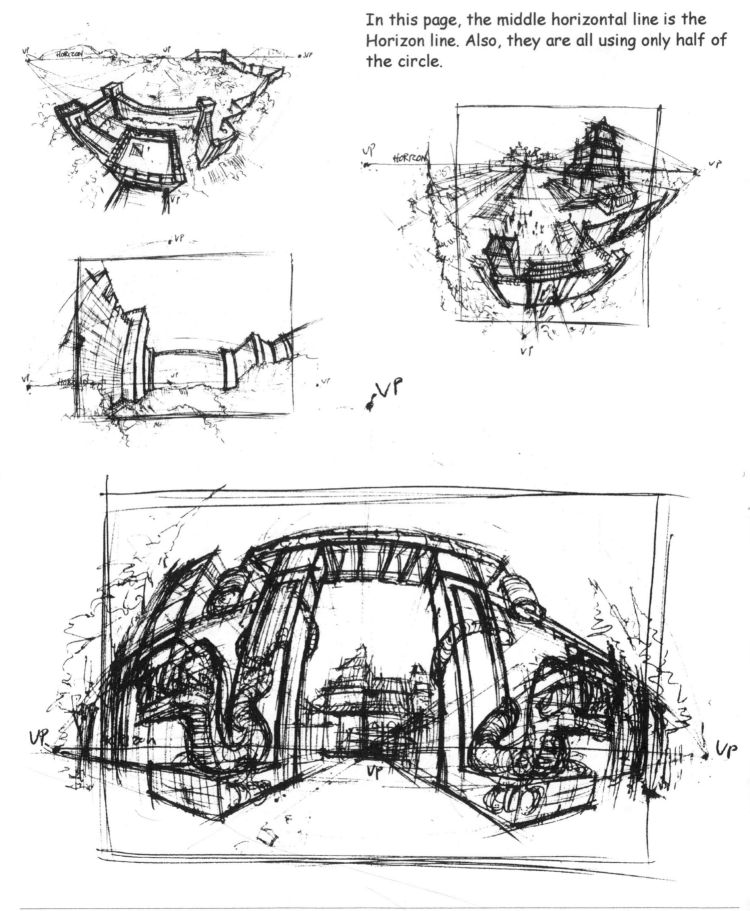

Fish-Eye

Nadir VP is in the middle

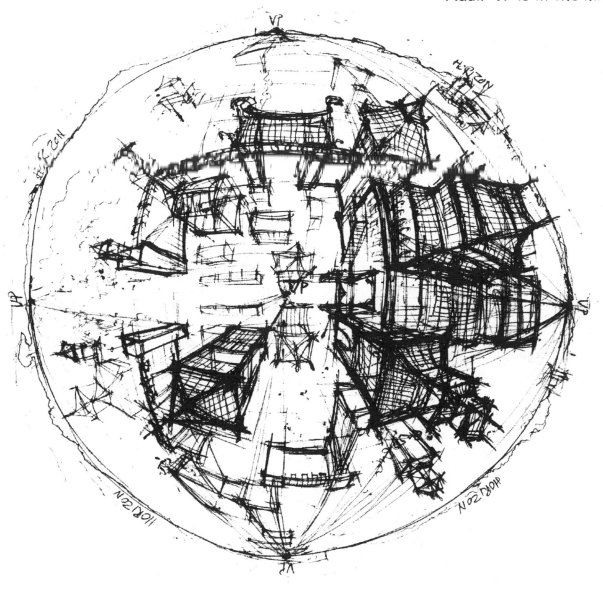

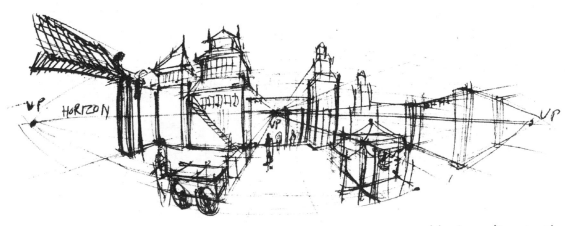

Horizon line in the middle

Creative Layout

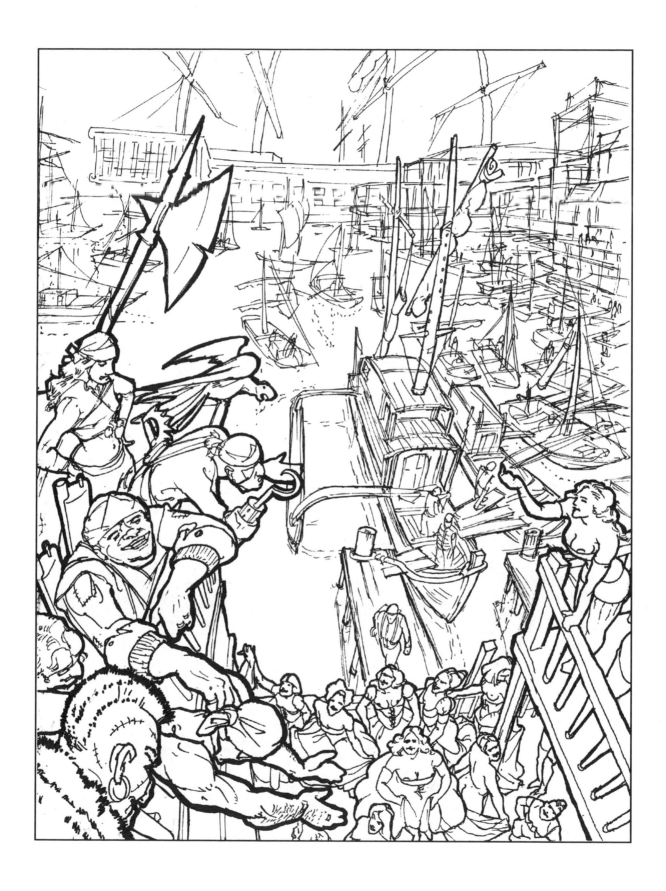

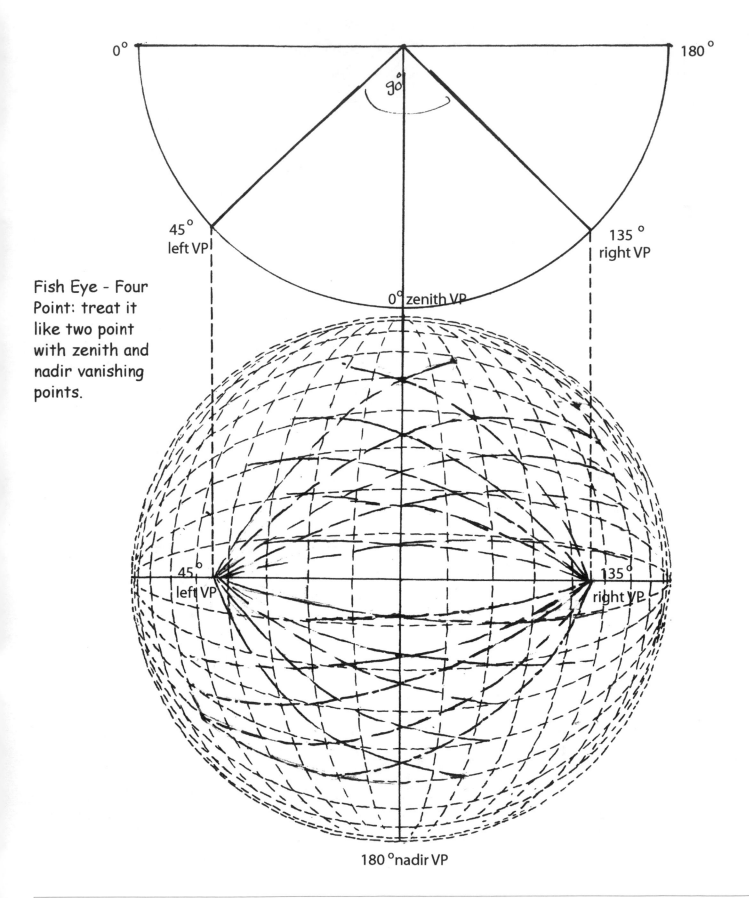

Fish Eye - Four Point: treat it like two point with zenith and nadir vanishing points.

Chapter 10

We can draw 360 degree angle Compositions (360 degree pivot) if zenith and nadir vanishing points are ignored.

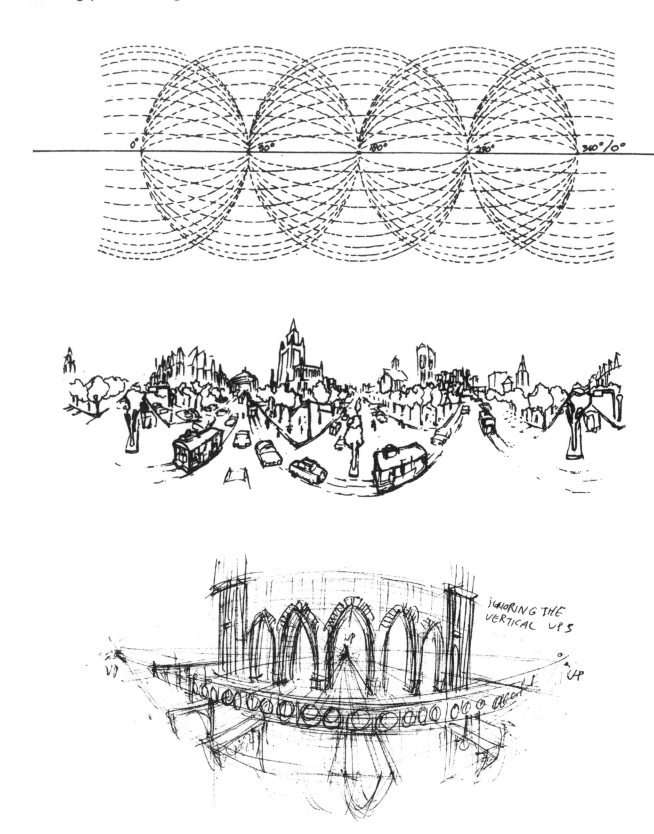

Not ignoring the zenith and nadir vanishing points can limit the artist view to only five planes in front of him. There's no way of drawing what's behind anymore.

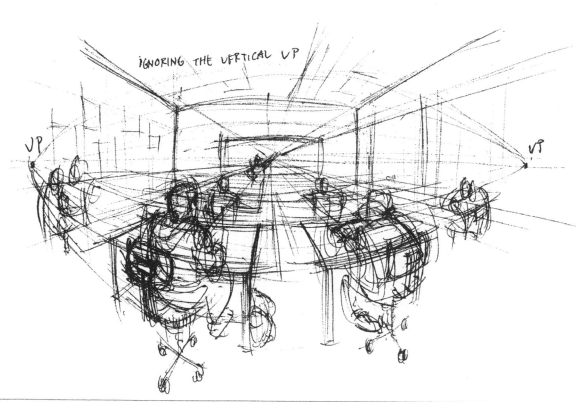

Chapter 10

To put light and shadow in a fish eye drawing, the artist should focus on form shadow rather than complex calculations of cast shadows.

Imagine complicated shapes as simple boxes.

Determent where the light is coming from.

Block all of the sides (in simple box shapes) that are not touching the light into shadow value.

Imagine the cast shadow of the object as if it was not in fish eye, than calculate it in to the fisheye grid. Block them in the same value as the form shadow.

Incorporate atmospheric perspective and darker cast shadow without sacrificing the value pattern and composition.

Creative Layout

Try the same steps with different sunlight and local light to convey mood and storytelling.

Simplifly your value pattern.

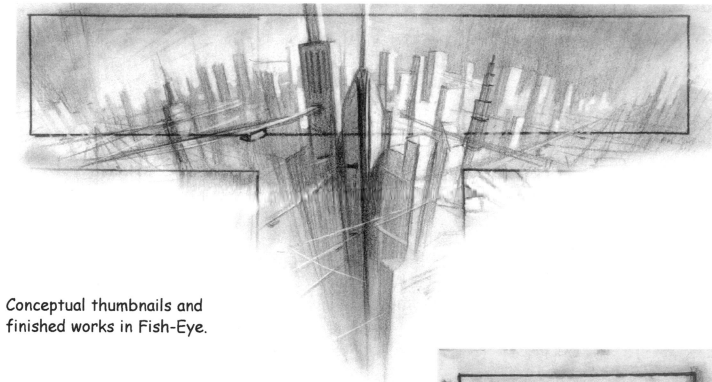

Conceptual thumbnails and finished works in Fish-Eye.

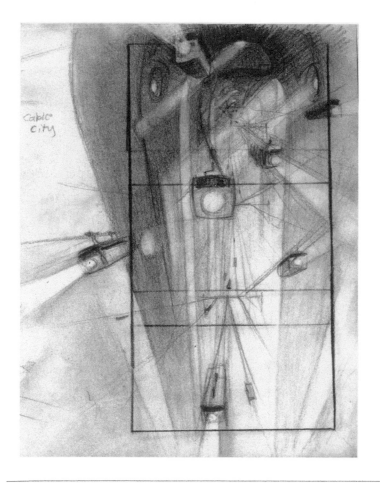

Chapter 11: Sequential Storytelling

Action...

Using Perspective in Sequential Storytelling

STORYBOARDS

Storyboards are sequential images using perspective, staging, composition and value to convey mood and get an idea or story across to the viewer. Storyboards are used as pre - production an pre - visualization work in movies, advertising, video game, web sites, 2D, 3D, animation.

Some things to keep in mind when doing storyboards:
*Keep your storytelling simple and straight to the point , by doing small thumbnails first and edit them
*Eliminate the superfluous and unnecessary and focus on the main important picture elements that will carry the story.
*Always establish where the story takes place with a establishing shot in the first frames, if in the middle of a scene your characters move to another location, re-establish the new location with another wide shot.
*Vary your camera angles constantly, avoiding a scene to become too stale.
*Use eye level views (most common), downshots (separates viewers from characters) upshots (engage viewers to characters), longshots, medium shorts and close ups (close ups only when needed, for expressing mood or objects too small to distinguish in other views).
*Establish light sources using value to create drama and mood to your story.
*The three most important things in animation are: anticipation, action and reaction.
*Keep it simple and clear!

Terms in Storyboarding

POV: point of view
CU: close up
WS: wide shot
MS: medium shot
SC: scene
FRM: frame
BG: background
OTS: over the shoulder
DS: downshot
US: upshot
EXT: exterior
INT: interior
PAN: panoramic view, camera moves side to side or up and down
CAM: camera
TRUCK IN: camera zooms in on a closer shot
TRUCK OUT: camera zooms out to a wider shot

Chapter 11

Long Shot - Establishing Shot

Eye Level Shot

Medium Shot

Upshot - Worm's Eye View

Close Up

Downshot - Bird's Eye View

180-DEGREE RULE (BREAKING THE AXIS)

The Axis is an imaginary line drawn between two characters, group of characters or even objects, as long as they are interacting with each other in an environment.
Draw the Axis on a top view of the characters in order to plan the positions of your camera.
As you can see in the example below, there's an 180 degree angle on both sides of the axis, place your camera on either side of the axis in the beginning of your shots, but make sure that you will keep it consistent by keeping the cam on the same side and not crossing the axis throughout the scene.
When you break the Axis from shot to shot during a scene, it will appear that your characters are trading places on the screen, confusing the audience.
Just as in any rule, there's always an exception, one of them is that you can cross the Axis if you show from shot to shot that the camera is "panning" around the character continuously.
Other than that keep the scene consistent by not breaking the Axis on every other frame.
As long as you choose one side of the Axis and keep the cam on that side, you can move the cam to any location you wish and at any distance or height from the characters.

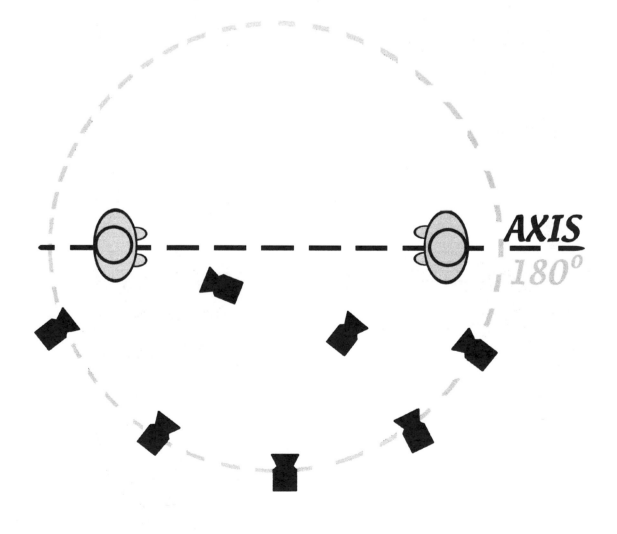

Chapter 11

Axis Sample

As you can see in this example, on the left side are the top view of the Cam, characters and the Axis; on the right side are the views from the different cameras.

Cam1 starts on one side of the Axis and then jumps to the other side in Cam2 (braking Axis), Cam3 and Cam4 are on the same side as Cam1.

On Views 1,3 and4, the camera flow is consistent, because even when the Cams change position in space, the characters remain on the same side of the screen, on the other hand, Cam2 breaks the consistency and flow of the scene by having characters A and B trading places on the screen.

Also think in terms of 'Screen Direction", if a character is going right for example, in frame one, don't show the character suddenly appearing to go left, because Cam is breaking the Axis. If you want to have a character turning to another direction, have a transition frame in between showing the character turning from one direction to another.

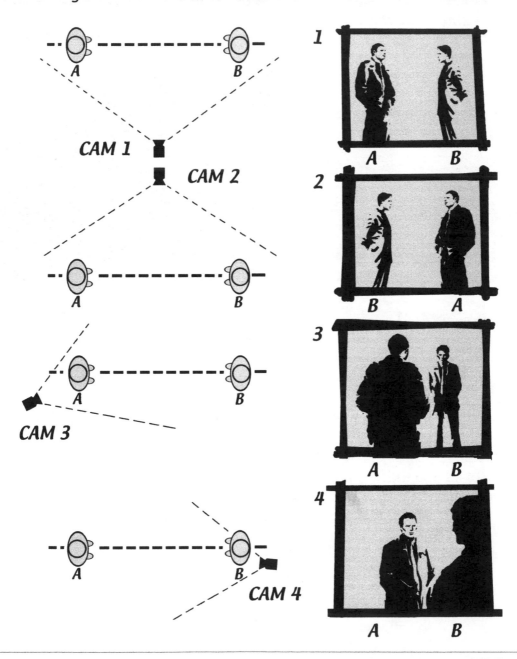

Truck Sequence

This is an example of a short sequence of a scene.
A monster truck is coming at us continuously frame by frame, there's little time elapsed from one frame to another, therefore we call it "Continuity Boards".
If my sequence consisted only of frames 1 and 4, which are the "Key frames" (main ideas) of this sequence, then we would have called it "Beat Boards".
Frame1 shows that there's something from a distance coming at us, and frame4 shows is a monster truck close to us and exiting the screen towards the right.
There's a substantial amount of time elapsed between 1 and 4, but it is still clear and straight to the point, using only the key ideas of the sequence.

THE DATE

Pantomime

The first 21 frames in this story are Beat Boards, Key frames with time elapsed in between focusing on the main ideas of a man waking up, getting a phone call, preparing himself for a date an getting late for it.

From frame 22 to the end, they are all continuity boards and also called "Pantomime Boards".

Pantomime Boards are when the camera is locked on the characters and everything is continuous and dialog and action are all explained in gestures, without word, focus on acting.

In this Case, the man is trying to come up with a story to his girlfriend as to why he was late, and of course it seems he wasn't really successful.

The style of these boards is cartoony, therefore you can use as many props and exaggerated poses as you want to get the story across.

Chapter 11

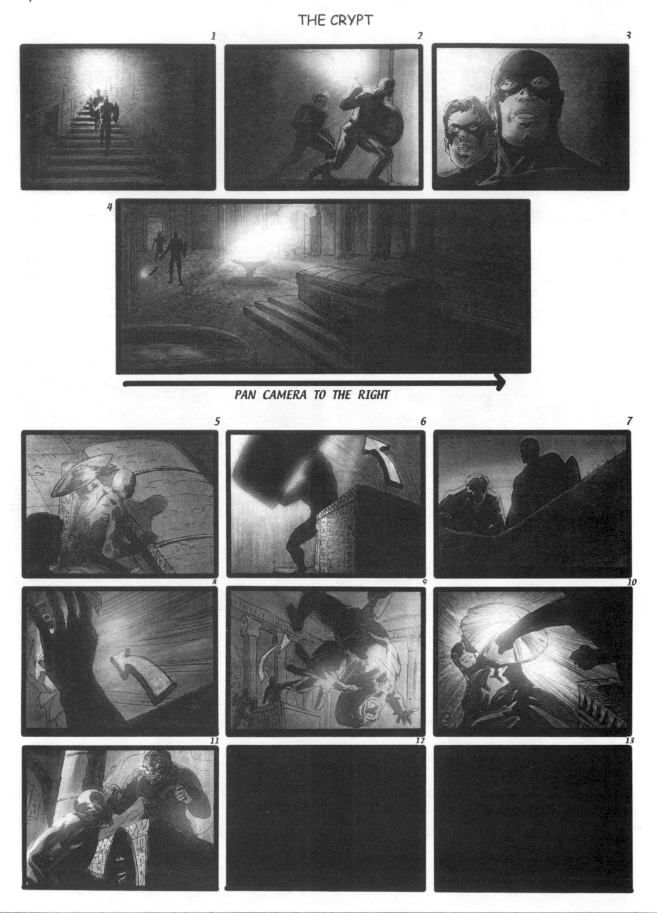

PAN CAMERA TO THE RIGHT

THE STALKER

The Stalker

This set of boards is all about design of strong silhouettes and simple black and white value to create drama.

Design strong silhouette poses with negative space that "reads" visually without relying on detail on the figure.

Try blacking out one of your poses with a thick marker, and see if the pose still "reads" if not, then... back to the drawing board!

Another thing about this set of boars besides the silhouette designs is that every frame follows the 180-degree rule and screen direction, except for frame 26, when the screen direction is broken on purpose.

Remember: anticipation, action and reaction.

In here we are building the anticipation to the audience, making them expect the stalker to appear on the left side of the screen, since we always show him on the left side. But we opted to break the screen direction and have the stalker surprisingly come from the right side (that's the action), and playoff the reaction of the character and the audience.

Since they traded places on frame 26, we will keep it consistent towards the end.

Chapter 11

Comic Books

In comic Books the same theories and techniques apply, except from one: Format/Layout.
In storyboards, formats vary, but the most common are frames measuring 4inches in
height by 5 inches wide, and always horizontal, except for vertical "Pan" shots.
In comics, pages are drawn in 11' by 17' boards containing anywhere from 1 to 8 frames
(panels) in it.
Try not to put more than 6 or 7 frames in each Comic page, as it will get too crowded.
Panels can be of any shape or size you can imagine, vertical or horizontal (the page itself
is always vertical).
But remember, we read from left to right and top to bottom, therefore make sure your
panels are placed or overlapped this way.
Be creative when designing the layout of your panels in a page, but at the same time keep
it simple and clear.
The viewer should be looking at your images in the proper order, instead of paying too
much attention to a fancy page layout.

Set 1 - Page Layout

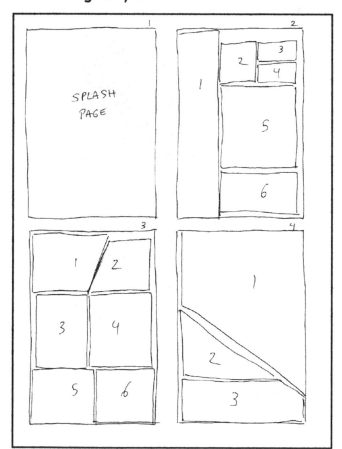

Set 2 - Page Layout

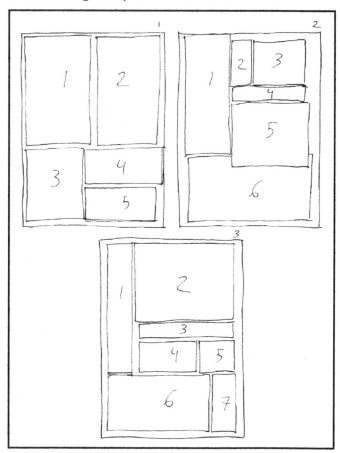

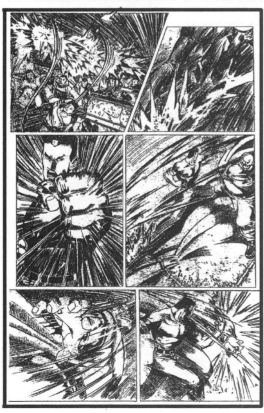

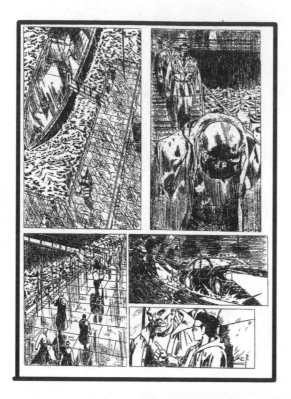

Here are some more layout samples of rough and finish Comic Book pages.
Have fun!!!

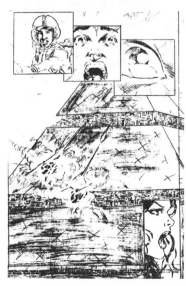

About the Authors:

Joko Budiono has worked in almost every single medium of art, and is still searching for that one perfect medium. He knew it was a lost cause, but did it anyway. " It is the search, not the work." He said once, quoting someone he could not remember. He hopes to continue this in the future, producing more, searching more and learning more.

Thomas Denmark has worked as an illustrator, designer and artist in various industries from graphic design in printing, product design, to concept and production art for video games. Some of his clients include Lucasarts (Totally Games), Electronic Arts, and Maxis.

Leandro Ng is an illustrator and storyboard artist, accomplished in both traditional and digital media. His versatile, yet distinctive style is reflected in an eclectic list of clients, which includes: Hasbro Toys, Levi Strauss, Gap Inc., San Francisco Opera House, Milesmall.com, Tepper & Kalmar Associates, Fancy Co. , Entity Comics, S.Q.P. Productions, Day One, Synergy, Third Degree Productions and Immortelle Studios, among others. Leandro also teaches Perspective at the Academy of Art in Northern California,. and makes his home in San Francisco.

BIBLIOGRAPHY

- Montague, John, Basic Perspective Drawing, Wiley.

- Pile, John, Perspective for Interior Designers, Whitney.

- Chelsea, David, Perspective for Comic Book Artists, Watson- Guptill.

- Watson, Ernest, How to use Creative Perspective, Dover.

- Etter, Howard, Perspective for Painters, Watson- Guptill.

- De Vries, Jan Vredeman, Perspective, Dover.